The Pocketbook Guide to Mental Health Act Assessments

Third edition

The Pocketbook Guide to Mental Health Act Assessments

Third edition

Claire Barcham

Mc Graw Hill Education

Open University Press

Open University Press
McGraw Hill
Unit 4
Foundation Park
Roxborough Way
Maidenhead
SL6 3UD

Email: emea_uk_ireland@mheducation.com
World wide web: www.mheducation.co.uk

Executive Editor: Sam Crowe
Editorial Assistant: Hannah Jones
Content Product Manager: Graham Jones

British Library Cataloguing in Publication Data
A catalogue record of this book is available from the British Library

ISBN-13: 9780335249138
ISBN-10: 0335249132
eISBN: 9780335249145

Typeset by Transforma Pvt. Ltd., Chennai, India

Praise for this book

"The undertaking of a Mental Health Act Assessment involves a wealth of statutory legislation, guidance, procedure, organisational process and system protocol. Each MHA assessment referral will require careful consideration by AMHPs and their multi-disciplinary colleagues to skilfully navigate the task in hand to address the health or safety or the safety of others in respect of the person concerned. This updated accessible pocketbook is a helpful addition for all practitioners and decision makers operating within the Mental Health Act process."

Jason Brandon, Mental Health Social Work Lead, Office of the Chief Social Worker for Adults, England, UK

"I am thrilled to include this book as a cornerstone text on all our CPD Mental Health Programme reading lists. Its remarkable strength lies in its ability to navigate the intricacies of the AMHP role with both practicality and simplicity. I eagerly anticipate our candidates delving into this text, as it promises to provide invaluable insight and guidance for AMHP practice."

Sandra Wilkinson, Senior Lecturer & Programme Lead in Advanced Mental Health Practice, UK

"I recommend this book without hesitation to anyone with a professional or personal interest in how the Mental Health Act works in practice. The book de-mystifies and unpicks the complexities of applying the Mental Health Act in the real world, leading the reader step by step through the process. The pocketbook is written so as to be accessible to a diverse audience, from students - AMHPs and other professionals – through to qualified and experienced AMHPs."

Dr David Watson, Principal Lecturer and Course Leader for the PG Dip Approved Mental Health Practice, University of Brighton, UK

"As an ex. ASW and currently a senior lecture on an AMHP programme I am more than happy to endorse this revised version of a much-read guide. Although slightly shorter than the 2nd edition, the revised structure is packed full of information and advice which guides the reader through the legislative process surrounding the considerations of assessment and support involved with MHA assessments. From the initial advice in the 3 bullet points to the introduction, what I used to refer to as the "put the kettle on moments" to the addition of appendices 7 (Autism) and 8 (135/136), this book is packed with hints and tips for practicing AMHP's, students and others to learn from and enjoy."

James Thomas, Co-Director and Senior Lecturer, Swansea University AMHP programme, UK

Contents

Acknowledgements   viii

List of abbreviations   ix

How to use this book   x

1   The legal landscape   1

2   Setting up Mental Health Act assessments   22

3   Managing Mental Health Act assessments and making decisions   80

4   Implementing decisions and admission to hospital   108

5   Working with compulsion in the community   131

Appendix 1   Local contacts for specialist groups of patients   159

Appendix 2   Admission to hospital: hospital managers' section
             papers checklist   161

Appendix 3   Sample reports, AMHP and Doctor   163

Appendix 4   The rights of the nearest relative   165

Appendix 5   Brief guide to assessing children and young people   168

Appendix 6   Brief guide to assessing rough sleepers   171

Appendix 7   Brief guide to assessing autistic people   174

Appendix 8   Brief guide to using S135 & 136   178

Glossary   181

References and useful resources   184

Index   185

Acknowledgements

I would like to express my gratitude to the following people: Jo Honigmann for contributing the section 'The Equality Act 2010'; Sarah Dewey for contributing the section 'The role and tasks of independent Mental Health Act advocates in MHA assessments'; Alison Greenhalgh and Shilpa Nairi for contributing the section 'Using crisis resolution or home treatment teams'; Alwyn Davies for providing work that is the basis of Chapter 4, 'Implementing decisions and admission to hospital'; Janet Blair in relation to Appendix 5; the authors of the Mental Health Service Interventions for Rough Sleepers in relation to Appendix 6; and Jill Corbyn, author of appendix 7 on assessing people on the Autistic spectrum.

List of abbreviations

AC	approved clinician
AMHP	approved mental health professional
BIA	best interest assessor
CAMHS	Child and Adolescent Mental Health Services
CMHT	community mental health team
CoP	Mental Health Act Code of Practice
CPN	community psychiatric nurse
CQC	Care Quality Commission
CRHT	crisis resolution/home treatment
CTO	community treatment order
DoLS	Deprivation of Liberty Safeguards
ECHR	European Convention on Human Rights
ECT	electroconvulsive therapy
EHRC	Equality and Human Rights Commission
GMC	General Medical Council
HRA	Human Rights Act 1998
ICB	Integrated Care Board
ICS	Integrated Care System
IMCA	independent mental capacity advocate
IMHA	independent mental health advocate
LPA	Lasting Power of Attorney
LSSA	local social service authority
MCA	Mental Capacity Act 2005
MHA	Mental Health Act 1983
MHRT	Mental Health Review Tribunal
NR	nearest relative
PR	parental responsibility
RC	responsible clinician
SOAD	second opinion appointed doctor

How to use this book

This handbook is aimed at approved mental health professionals and other professionals working in mental health services such as doctors, nurses and occupational therapists. It may also be helpful to others, such as police officers, who are often involved in Mental Health Act (MHA) assessments. It aims to provide a quick and easy guide to MHA assessments and the legal frameworks within which they take place.

The book is designed to 'lead you through' the process of deciding whether to set up, arrange, and undertake an MHA assessment. Each chapter begins with a summary of what will be covered and includes features such as examples from practice, checklists, and reminder boxes, concluding with another summary. A glossary at the back of the book provides definitions of key terms, which are emboldened in the text where they first appear. A list of commonly used abbreviations is included for ready reference, and references and resources you can make use of in practice can be found at the back of the book.

The following icons are used to highlight particular features:

✓ Checklist

⚖ Quote from legal material, usually the Mental Health Act 1983 or the Reference Guide to the Mental Health Act[1]

💡 Remember! – key information to remember

📖 Information relating to the Mental Health Act Code of Practice

! Key issue

When the book talks about 'the Mental Health Act' or 'MHA', it is referring to the Mental Health Act 1983, as amended by the Mental Health Act 2007. When 'the Code of Practice', 'the Code' or 'the CoP' are used, these refer to the 2015 version of the Code of Practice to the Mental Health Act 1983.

People subject to MHA assessments must be or appear to be suffering from a mental disorder. In the Mental Health Act they are defined as 'patients'. The predecessor of the approved mental health professional (**AMHP**) was the approved social worker and in social work the term 'service user' (and prior to that 'client') was used to reflect a more positive and active role of a person involved in, and able to direct, their own care or treatment, rather than being the passive recipient of 'treatment'. In this book, the term 'patient' is usually used simply to follow the legal definition of the person as set out in the Mental Health Act.

Note

1 Published by the Department of Health, this book accompanies the Code of Practice to the Mental Health Act, and provides practical information about how to understand the Act. For example, the rules around when mistakes on recommendations or applications can be amended can be found in the Reference Guide as opposed to the Code of Practice.
https://www.gov.uk/government/publications/code-of-practice-mental-health-act-1983 and Reference Guide: https://www.gov.uk/government/publications/mental-health-act-1983-reference-guide

1 The legal landscape

This chapter looks at the legal framework within which decisions about people's mental health need to be made. It sets the context for the book as a whole, and aims to help professionals be clear about the decisions that need to be made and the legal basis for those decisions. This third edition has been updated to take account of the changes to s135 and s136.

By the end of the chapter, you should have an understanding of:

- Human rights and equality legislation, and how they contribute to the framework for decision-making concerning an individual's mental health
- The Mental Capacity Act 2005, its Codes of Practice, and its contributions to the care and treatment of people with mental health problems
- The Children Act 1989 and other legislation relating to the care and treatment of children and young people
- The Mental Health Act 1983, and the relationship between this Act and the Mental Capacity Act 2005 when making decisions about the care and treatment of people with mental health problems

Introduction

Everyone has certain rights, including the right to personal freedom and to private and family life. They also have the right to expect that professionals will uphold those rights. So whenever as professionals we are thinking about intervening in a person's life, it is only right to start by asking ourselves some key questions.

- What is it I feel I need to do?
- Why do I feel I need to do it?
- Who is giving me the authority to intervene here?

In many cases, it will be the person themselves who provides the authority by asking for or agreeing to the help they need. However, mental health is one area of practice where we are more likely to need a formal legal framework in order to provide authority for our interventions.

For people who lack **capacity** to make decisions about their mental health, the Mental Capacity Act 2005 (MCA) may provide the protection that is needed. For most adults who need help with their mental health problems, but refuse intervention, the Mental Health Act 1983 (MHA) provides the legal framework to detain, assess and treat someone against their will. For children and young people, the situation can be more complex, with parental authority providing additional sources of authority upon which professionals may rely.

This chapter aims to help professionals understand how these different frameworks work together, and how to make choices between them. It aims to help you understand when to support people to make their own decisions about their care, and when the state – in the form of AMHPs, doctors and other professionals – can and should intervene.

The effect of the Human Rights Act 1998 on mental health legislation

The Human Rights Act 1998 (HRA) works by imposing a duty on 'public authorities' (NHS Trusts, local authorities and the employees of these organisations are all 'public authorities') to only 'act in a way' that is compatible with the European Convention on Human Rights ((ECHR) (section 6 (1)). This is further defined in section 3 of the HRA in the following manner: *'So far as it is possible to do so, primary legislations and subordinate legislation must be read and given effect in a way which is compatible with Convention rights.'* In effect, the law tells the courts to interpret the MHA and all other forms of legislation in ways that, wherever possible, are compatible with 'human rights'. However, Parliament was careful to reserve for itself the ability to amend **primary legislation** that wasn't compatible. The courts can only reach a decision that it is impossible for them to interpret a piece of legislation in a manner that would be human rights compliant, and rule that a particular Act or section of an Act is incompatible.

> ### Remember!
>
> AMHPs are 'public authorities' because a) they have powers that a private body or citizen would not normally have (see *Aston Cantlow* [2004] 1 AC 546); and b) they carry out functions in their role which are 'of a public nature' (HRA s6(3)). Because of this status, AMHPs have particular duties not only under the HRA, but also the Equality Act 2010 and the Freedom of Information Act 2000. They must also abide by public law requirements of fairness, reasonableness and lawfulness.

Articles 5 (the right to liberty), 3 (the right not to be treated in an inhumane or degrading manner) and 8 (the right to private and family life) are particularly relevant to the Mental Health Act assessment process.

How does the HRA work?

'The State' (and those who intervene in people's lives on behalf of the state, such as AMHPs and doctors) is expected to act in ways that comply with the articles of the ECHR. This means not doing things that infringe people's rights *and* positively intervening to ensure people have access to those rights.

Remember!

There are 66 articles, but not all relate to mental health. There are also a number of protocols, not all of which have been ratified in the UK.

The Convention was conceived as a 'living' document that would develop through **case law** and, as society changed, new case law interpretations would emerge to meet people's needs. This was different from the way domestic British courts acted before the HRA, where the expectation had been that new case law must reflect previous decisions unless Parliament intervened and legislated differently. However, since the introduction of the HRA, courts in the UK are expected to balance the desire for continuity with the duty to interpret legislation in an ECHR-compatible manner.

Example from practice

What should be meant by 'deprivation of liberty' (Article 5) has been closely scrutised in many legal cases since the introduction of the Deprivation of Liberty Safeguards in 2009. This resulted in a Supreme Court ruling in March 2014[1], which gave the definition as being 'under continuous supervision and control, and not free to leave'. This definition has had a significant impact in understanding in many areas of practice, not least when thinking about making decisions under the MHA.

The Article rights are universal (which means they apply to everyone) but not all of them are absolute; some, as with Article 5, are qualified. This means that reasons are given about the situations where they may not apply. Rights often have to be balanced against one another, such as balancing the individual's rights to private family life, and other people's rights to safety and security and Article 5 recognises this.

Article 5

1   No one shall be deprived of his liberty save in the following cases and in accordance with a procedure prescribed by law:

    (e) the lawful detention ... of persons of unsound mind ...

> 2 Everyone who is arrested shall be informed promptly, in a language which he understands, of the reasons for his arrest and any charges against him.
>
> ECHR

Equality Act 2010[2]

The Equality Act 2010 brings previous discrimination legislation (such as the Race Relations Act 1976, the Sex Discrimination Act 1975 and the Disability Discrimination Act 1995) under one statute for England, Wales and Scotland. Northern Ireland has separate discrimination legislation. The Equality and Human Rights Commission (the 'EHRC') has produced several statutory codes of practice and corresponding technical and non-statutory guidance which can be found on its website. Of most relevance to AMHPs are the Code of Practice on Services, Public Functions and Associations (which should be read in conjunction with a Supplement first published by the EHRC on 31 March 2014 and updated in May 2014) together with the equivalent non-statutory guidance and the Technical Guidance for the Public Sector Equality Duty, for which there are separate publications for England, Scotland and Wales.

Under the Equality Act 2010, people are protected from discrimination and harassment in different contexts based on their protected characteristics. In relation to the provision of goods, facilities and services and the exercise of public functions the protected characteristics are as follows: age (for people aged 18 and over), disability, gender reassignment, pregnancy and maternity, race, religion or belief, sex and sexual orientation. Victimisation is also unlawful.

AMHPs owe duties towards individuals with protected characteristics who are using or trying to use a service both when acting in a service provider role as a nurse, social worker, occupational therapist or psychologist for example, and when acting as an AMHP, that is when carrying out a public function. AMHPs are also subject to the general public sector equality duty under s149 of the Equality Act 2010 when carrying out a public function, which means they have to give due regard to the need to:

> a eliminate discrimination, harassment, victimisation and any other conduct that is prohibited by or under [the] Act;
>
> b advance equality of opportunity between persons who share a protected characteristic and persons who do not share it;
>
> c foster good relations between persons who share a relevant protected characteristic and persons who do not share it.
>
> s149(1) Equality Act 2010

Equality principles as reflected in the Equality Act 2010 tie in closely with the five overarching principles of the MHA Code of Practice (CoP).

The Mental Capacity Act 2005: its influences on the care and treatment of people with mental health problems

The Mental Capacity Act 2005 (MCA) took what were formerly **common law** rules about the liberty, care and treatment of people who lack capacity (either temporarily or permanently) and used them as a basis to introduce comprehensive new legislation. The starting point of the legislation, as the Act's title suggests, is that all adults over the age of 16 years are presumed to have the capacity to make decisions for themselves unless or until it can be demonstrated that they lack capacity to do so in a particular situation. Supporting people wherever possible to make their own decisions, and being involved in the decision-making process even where they don't have capacity for all decisions, is a central theme.

Definitions

Whereas the criteria for the Mental Health Act means it can apply to anyone with 'any disorder of the mind' (s1), the Mental Capacity Act applies to anyone with 'an impairment of, or a disturbance in the functioning of the mind or brain' (S2 MCA). In practice, what this means is that the Mental Health Act would normally not apply to someone who had a disorder associated solely with the brain (for example, people suffering from a stroke, or in a persistent vegetative state) unless that disorder of the brain resulted in a mental disorder. Many more people, therefore, potentially come within the remit of the MCA than MHA.

Age requirements

The MCA applies to everyone over the age of 16 who lacks capacity to make specific decisions for themselves, *except* that a 16- or 17-year-old cannot make **advance decisions** or nominate or be nominated as having a **Lasting Power of Attorney (LPA)** until they are 18 years old. Additionally, **Deprivation of Liberty Safeguards (DoLS)** procedures cannot be used for anyone under the age of 18. However, the **Liberty Protection Safeguards (LPS)** when/if they replace DoLS will be available to those aged 16 years or older.

The impact of the MCA legislation on people who, for example, have a learning disability or a degenerative illness such as dementia, has been clearly appreciated. The manner in which this legislation impacts on the care of people with mental health problems, whose capacity may fluctuate, and the MHA assessment process is also significant.

This section seeks to focus on the key concepts of the Act and apply them to the assessment and care of people with mental health problems. More detail about the MCA in general can be found in the Code of Practice to that Act, as well as the companion book in this series, *The Pocketbook Guide to Mental Capacity Act Assessments*.

Key concepts

- The principles of the MCA (s1);
- The meaning of a lack of capacity;
- Responsibility for testing capacity;
- The 'best interests' checklist;
- Protection from **liability** under section 5 and the limitations on section 5 imposed by section 6;
- Advance decisions and their applicability to mental health practice and care and to refuse treatment;
- The role and function of a donee of a Lasting Power of Attorney (an 'attorney');
- The role of the **Court of Protection**, and in particular its power to appoint a **deputy**;
- The role and function of **Independent Mental Capacity Advocates (IMCAs)**;
- The safeguards and the procedure for authorising deprivation of liberty;
- Informal treatment under the Mental Health Act and capacity issues.

The principles of the MCA

1   A person must be assumed to have capacity unless it is established that he lacks capacity;

2   A person is not to be treated as unable to make a decision unless all practicable steps to help him to do so have been taken without success;

3   A person is not to be treated as unable to make a decision merely because he makes an unwise decision;

4   An act done, or decision made, under this Act for or on behalf of a person who lacks capacity must be done, or made, in his best interests;

5   Before the act is done, or the decision is made, regard must be had to whether the purpose for which it is needed can be as effectively achieved in a way that is less restrictive of the person's rights and freedom of action.

s1 Mental Capacity Act 2005

These principles appear on the face of the Act, and influence all the subsequent legislation and procedures that follow. It means, for example, that having a diagnosis of schizophrenia allows no presumption that someone lacks capacity to make decisions or, if they make a decision that we feel is unwise, that this would always be 'evidence' of incapacity. A more balanced approach that takes account both of the possibility that actions may be related to mental ill heath as well as the possibility that they are not, is needed.

Consider the following example.

Example from practice

Gerry has inherited £17,000. He wishes to give £5,000 to his brother (who visits rarely and staff feel has little interest in him) and spend the remainder on new musical equipment. Staff are concerned that the stress of having to handle the money is exacerbating his schizophrenic illness and feel that he should save the money and that his brother doesn't 'deserve' to have anything.

Gerry explains that he appreciates that the money is unlikely to change his relationship with his brother, but that he has in the past destroyed his brother's property when unwell, and wants to make amends. On reflection, staff realise that, although they do not agree with Gerry's decision, his mental health problems are not affecting his capacity to decide whether or not to make the gift to his brother, and that he is within his rights to do so.

How mental capacity is defined

A person lacks capacity in relation to a decision or proposed intervention if, at the material time, he is unable to make a decision for himself in relation to the matter or proposed intervention because of an impairment of, or a disturbance in the functioning of the mind or brain. It does not matter whether the impairment or disturbance is permanent or temporary.

s2 (1) and (2) MCA

The key point about the definition used is that it has two points or stages:

- Point one is establishing that the person has an impairment of, or disturbance in the functioning of, the mind or brain.
- Point two is that as a consequence of this impairment or disturbance they are unable to make the decision at the time that it needs to be made.

Remember!

The important thing about the definition is that it makes it clear that someone can have an 'impairment or disturbance in the mind or brain' yet that may not have any impact on decision-making at a particular point in time, and conversely, a person may be unable to make a decision for reasons unrelated to such an impairment or disturbance. For example, decision-making can be undermined by other people putting pressure on an individual – this may be an offence, but it may not indicate a lack of mental capacity to make the decision.

Testing for capacity to make decisions: the four-step test in s3 MCA

A person is unable to make a decision for himself if he is unable to:

1 understand the information relevant to the decision;
2 retain that information long enough to reach a decision;
3 use or weigh that information as part of the process of making the decision; or
4 communicate his decision (whether by talking, using sign language, visual aids or any other means).

Note that the decision is 'time specific' and 'issue specific'. It is also a test applied both to people with temporary or fluctuating capacity (such as people experiencing mental health crisis) and those whose decision-making is permanently impaired (such as people with a learning disability). If a person cannot fulfil any of the first three points above they are unable to make the decision. The fourth point only applies where a person cannot communicate their decision in any way.

Responsibility for testing capacity

Responsibility for testing a person's capacity rests with the person who wishes to intervene in their lives, to make a decision on their behalf or to intervene to provide care or support. Clearly, less complex decisions (such as what someone might wear for the day) need less scrutiny than complex decisions which will have significant repercussions (such as whether someone should move permanently into residential care) but the basic concept is the same.

Example from practice

While on AMHP duty, Jerry is phoned by a GP and ambulance crew. The GP asks Jerry to organise an urgent Mental Health Act assessment because the older woman she has just seen has a suspected urinary tract infection, is confused and aggressive and is refusing to get into the ambulance. Jerry explains to the GP that she needs to make an assessment of whether the woman has the capacity to make the decision not to go into hospital, and if she does not have the capacity, the Ambulance staff will need to decide whether the restraint needed to enable them to convey the woman would be proportionate to the risks she would face if they didn't take her to hospital. They would also need to be satisfied that it would be in the woman's best interests to be taken to hospital.

Best interests checklist at s4 MCA

The best interests checklist represents the issues that should be considered when decisions or interventions are made on behalf of someone who lacks capacity, if the decisions (and the decision maker) are to be protected by the MCA.

> ## Remember!
>
> The person that wishes to intervene or make a decision on behalf of someone else must have a reasonable belief, based on the evidence of the case, that the person lacks the capacity to make that decision or to agree to the needed intervention, and must be working in the person's best interests when intervening.

The checklist items include that the decision maker:

- must not make their judgement based merely on the person's age, appearance, condition (or diagnosis);
- must take into account whether the person is likely to regain capacity with regard to the decision in hand, and whether the decision can wait;
- must as far as reasonably practicable, 'permit and encourage' the person to communicate, including by acting to improve their ability to communicate (for example, by using an advocate);
- must not, where the decision relates to life-sustaining treatment, be motivated by a desire to bring about their death;
- must so far as is possible consider the person's past wishes and any preferences (particularly when written down) stated by them when they had capacity;
- must take account of the beliefs and values that would have been likely to influence their decision had they had capacity;
- must, if practical and appropriate, consult anyone previously named by the patient as someone who should be consulted, any carers, anyone who has a relevant LPA – a 'donee' (remembering that there are two kinds of LPA – (i) personal welfare, and (ii) property and affairs), and any appointed court deputy about their views concerning what would be in the person's best interests.

> ## Remember!
>
> Best interest decision-making is less about what professionals or even family members think might be the right decision, and more about what the person themselves might have wanted to do, had they had capacity to make the decision.

Protection from liability under s5 of the MCA

The MCA is also different from the MHA in that it doesn't provide authority to intervene in people's lives; rather it provides legal protection for people who need to intervene in the lives of people who lack capacity so that they are able to make a decision on that person's behalf, or provide the care the person needs, as long as they have a reasonable belief that the person lacks capacity to make the particular decision and they are working in the person's best interests.

Protection from liability is limited, however, in situations where decisions about major life changes are involved, or where the care needed would amount to a deprivation of the person's liberty, or where you wish to take money from a person's bank account or sell property. In such cases, special rules have been developed (see the Code of Practice to the MCA for more information on this).

Generally, however, protection is available as long as:

- reasonable steps have been taken to gain permission from the person concerned;
- you are reasonably sure the person lacks the capacity to make a particular decision;
- you are working in their best interests, and before making the intervention you have considered a 'less restrictive' option than the one proposed, and only ruled it out because it is less effective than the one you are now taking;
- if restraint is needed, it is a proportionate response to the risk of harm to the person themselves if no action is taken;
- the action doesn't amount to a deprivation of liberty, or conflict with an advance decision made by the person, their LPA or a deputy;
- you are spending money to buy goods or pay for services that are in the person's best interests.

Key issue

When the House of Lords[3] reviewed the working of the Mental Capacity Act in 2014, they were particularly critical of the way professionals were using the Act. 'For many who are expected to comply with the Act it appears to be an optional add-on, far from being central to their working lives ... The prevailing cultures of paternalism (in health) and risk aversion (in social care) have prevented the Act from becoming widely known or embedded.'

Limitations to s5 by s6 MCA

There are a number of limitations placed on the protection offered by s5 of the MCA.

Life-changing events. Decisions about life-changing events, such as changes in residence and serious medical treatment will only be covered under s5 if the decision maker/s first consult all appropriate parties, and secondly consider whether there is a less restrictive way in which the care/treatment needed can be given. If there is no one that professionals can consult in these specific circumstances, an **independent mental capacity advocate** (IMCA) must be instructed to assess whether they agree that your plan will be in the best interests of the person concerned.

> ### Remember!
>
> If you are working with someone with long term mental health needs, and are considering a long term residential or hospital placement for them, if you believe they lack capacity to take the decision to move for themselves, you must consult any friends and relatives involved in their care, and if they have no such contacts, an IMCA must be involved in the decision-making process.

Depriving someone of their liberty in a hospital or care home (registered under part II of the Care Standards Act). Where the care that someone needs would amount to a deprivation of their liberty, this would not be protected under section 5, and legal authority for this deprivation must be obtained. In the majority of cases, if a patient with a mental disorder needs to be detained for assessment or treatment, the Mental Health Act will need to be used. See Chapter 6 for more details on situations where The Mental Capacity Act Deprivation of Liberty Safeguards (DoLS) might apply.

> ### Remember!
>
> The Supreme Court decided in March 2014 that 'Deprivation of Liberty' meant 'being under continuous supervision, and control, and not free to leave.'
>
> (see note 1 for details)

Depriving someone of their liberty in places other than a hospital or registered care home. 'Community DoLS'. If the care someone needs amounts to deprivation of liberty and it is occurring in places other than a hospital or registered care home, currently the DoLS will not be available. Such care could only be authorised by an order of the Court of Protection. Since November 2014, a process mirroring the DoLS process but approved by the Court of Protection has been available.[4] However, if in the future the LPS come into force, they will apply in all settings. (So in people's homes, in shared housing as well as care homes or hospitals, the LPS will be available in future.)

The legal frameworks for the care and treatment of children and young people who have mental health problems

Just as with decisions concerning adults, when working with children and young people experiencing mental health problems, a good place to start is by asking yourself: what is it that I feel I need to do? And on whose authority am I doing it? The difference, however, is that depending on the age of the child or young person, there are differences in the legal frameworks that exist and which can be used to justify intervention.

The MHA (with the exception of **guardianship**, s7) has no age limits so may also be available as a legal framework in circumstances where the child has a mental disorder, and also meets the other criteria for use of the Act.

The Children Act 1989 or the MHA?

The Children Act s25, although it does provide authority in certain circumstances to detain a child, provides no authority to enforce assessment or treatment. The key question is the purpose of the intervention. If assessment or treatment for a mental disorder is needed, then the MHA may be more appropriate. However, if the child is behaving in a challenging manner and does not need assessment or treatment for a mental disorder, the Children Act 1989 may be a more appropriate framework, provided the s25 criteria (which allow a child or young person to be deprived of their liberty in a secure children's home) are met. There are, however, significant concerns about the availability of secure accommodation, and whether such homes are able to provide the therapeutic care that many young people need.

Deprivation of Liberty and under-18-year-olds

The case of 'D' in 2015 (see endnote 5) established that the Supreme Court definition of 'deprivation of liberty' should apply as much to those under 18 as it does to those over 18. When considering whether a DoL is occurring, the key test is whether the restrictions needed are significantly different from those any other child or young person of a similar age might experience. Therefore, if care needs to be provided to someone under 18 in a way that is significantly more restrictive than would be the case for a child of a similar age, but without additional needs, this could amount to a deprivation of their liberty and a legal framework must be found to authorise that deprivation.

Using parental responsibility (PR) to authorise a deprivation of liberty. Case law tells us that a parent with PR can agree to a number of restrictions to protect a child they are responsible for, and can also authorise a deprivation of liberty for an under-16-year-old in some circumstances.[5] In the 'D'[6] case from March 2015, Mr Justice Keehan in the family Courts decided that the parents of an autistic 15-year-old boy who lacked capacity could authorise the deprivation of his liberty required to provide the care he needed, but recognised that once he turned 16, this would be a matter for the Court of Protection, not the parents. This position was subsequently endorsed by the Supreme Court, on the basis that D's parents were working in his best interests, there were no concerns about their decision-making, and D himself lacked capacity and did not object to the care provided.

Other legal frameworks available to authorise deprivation of liberty for an under-18-year-old. So although it has been accepted that the Supreme Court definition of what a deprivation of liberty means does apply to under-18-year-olds, the DoLS safeguards themselves are not available to this group. Where there are concerns that the care or treatment that is needed will deprive an under-18-year-old of their liberty, either the courts need to be approached or the Mental Health Act needs to be used to provide the authority required.

Can the local authority use its PR to authorise a deprivation of liberty? The Re D case (and other subsequent cases) also raised the issue of whether the local authority of a child in care (or the child's parents in such situations) can use their parental responsibility to authorise a deprivation of liberty. Here the Courts have been very clear: a local authority who has PR by virtue of an interim or full care order *cannot* authorise a deprivation of liberty; this authority must come from the Courts or from other legal mechanisms.

In July 2022, the Family Division of the High Court in England opened a national deprivation of liberty court (based at the Royal Courts of Justice) to take all new applications to deprive under-18-year-olds of their liberty, using the inherent jurisdiction of the High Court.

In its first 12 months the court considered cases related to 1249 children. This compares with under 300 applications for secure accommodation during the same period.

Children subject to deprivation of liberty orders,
Nuffield Family Justice Observatory 2023

Remember!

The Human Rights Act 1998 and Equality Act 2010 apply equally to children and young people as they do to adults.

The scope of parental responsibility

Where we are dealing with children under the age of 16, and those aged 16 or 17 who lack capacity, those with parental responsibility may be able to provide authority for assessment and treatment provided the decision is within the 'scope of parental responsibility'[7]. This term is used in the MHA Code of Practice Chapter 19, to describe the types of decisions that parents will be able to make in relation to their child's care and treatment for mental disorder.

Key factors to consider when thinking about whether a decision falls within the 'scope' include:

• Whether the child/young person has competence or capacity. If they do, it would be unwise to rely on PR (and illegal if the child is aged 16 or 17).

- Whether this is a decision another parent of a similarly aged child would reasonably expect to be able to make. If the decision involves a particularly invasive treatment, such as ECT for example, it would be unwise to rely on PR.
- Whether there are any concerns about a parent's ability to make decisions, for example because they lack capacity themselves, or they are finding it difficult to focus on the child's best interests. If in doubt, seek further advice!

The overall effect of the scope is that it provides a way of deciding when parental authority will provide 'enough' authority, and when to consider the Mental Health Act instead.

Example from practice

Sophie, 13 years old, was admitted after her weight dropped below a previously agreed 'safe' level. She was very resistant about eating and had previously pulled out a feeding tube causing damage to her throat. She was not felt to be **Gillick competent**. The question was therefore whether her parents could decide on the treatment on her behalf.

Her parents were unhappy about the idea of using the Mental Health Act, and said they would authorise staff to hold her down at meal times and force feed her.

However, staff were unhappy with this approach, and agreed that because the treatment needed was invasive, the decision fell outside of the 'scope of parental responsibility' and the use of the MHA should be considered instead.

Summary of frameworks for under-18-year-olds

For children aged under 16, either the child themselves (if they are Gillick competent) or the person or people who have parental responsibility for them (if they are not Gillick competent, and the decision falls within the scope of PR) can provide the authority needed to admit, assess or treat the child for their mental disorder. If the admission amounts to a deprivation of liberty, particularly if the child is Gillick competent, it would be unwise to rely on the authority of someone with PR. It is also not possible to use the local authorities' PR to authorise the deprivation, for a child or young person on a full or interim care order.

Young people aged 16 or 17 years old are covered by the MCA (with some minor exceptions) so are presumed to have capacity to make decisions, including making decisions about admission, assessment or treatment for a mental disorder. Additionally, the MHA s131 makes it clear that 16- and 17-year-olds who have capacity and object to admission to hospital cannot be admitted on the basis of parental authority. If admission is thought necessary, whether they fit the criteria for admission using the MHA Act s2 or s3 would need to be considered.

> It is most unlikely that there will be any place for informal admission for inca-
> pacitated 16/17 year olds on the basis of parental consent.
>
> Alex Ruck-Keene & Xinyu Xu
> Medical Law Review, Vol. 0, No. 0, pp. 1–10 doi:10.1093/medlaw/fwaa007

The relationship between informal treatment under s131 of the MHA, s5 and s6 of the MCA and Mental Health Act Assessments

S131 of the Mental Health Act provides the legal basis for people to be admitted to hospital informally. It also makes it clear that a young person aged 16 or 17 can choose to be admitted informally, but cannot be made to come into hospital by their parents if they object.

However, the rules are slightly different depending on whether or not the person has capacity to decide on admission and treatment. If the person has capacity, they can be admitted informally as long as they understand what would be involved, and they consent. This includes agreeing to be assessed or treated in a way that would amount to a deprivation of their liberty.

If a person lacks capacity, they can be admitted informally as long as they do not object, and will not be deprived of their liberty. This is because s5 and s6 of the MCA only provide protection as long as care or treatment does not amount to a deprivation of their liberty. In reality, the 2014 Supreme Court judgement means that *in most cases, an admission to hospital for assessment or treatment of a mental disorder will almost always amount to a deprivation of liberty, and will need to be authorised by the law.*

Advance decisions to refuse medical treatment

It is important to recognise the difference between advance decisions to refuse medical treatment and advance statements. Advance decisions to refuse medical treatment allow a person to object in advance to particular sorts of medical treatment or intervention (such as objecting to ECT). Such decisions, as long as they are specific to the situation and were made at a time when the person had capacity, are legally binding. However, they may be overridden by the use of the MHA (except where they object to ECT – see below). **Advance statements** allow people to say what they would like to happen in given situations, for example, asking that particular people are consulted or involved during a Mental Health Act assessment. However, they are not legally binding.

People with mental health problems have the same rights as others to make advance decisions about their medical treatment, provided that the decisions were made when they had the capacity to make them. The decision must be *valid and applicable.*

To be *valid* an advance decision must be made by a person who:

- is 18 years or older;
- had capacity to make the specific decision at the time they made it.

To be *applicable* the decision must be relevant to a given situation.

The decision is better if it is explicit rather than general, so that it can easily be applied to a given situation (for example, refusing to have a particular type of antipsychotic medication).

The advance decision doesn't have to be written down for it to be valid, unless it involves the refusal of life-sustaining treatment – in which case it must:

- be in writing;
- be signed;
- be witnessed;
- clearly state that the decision applies even if life is at risk.

Care must be taken when helping people experiencing mental ill health to make a valid advance decision, because:

- the person concerned has to have had capacity when the decision was made;
- and the advance decision has to be available to people who might be called upon to make a decision in an urgent situation such as an assessment under the Mental Health Act.

It is helpful for issues such as this to be considered early, when planning someone's care and support with them, so that confirmation of capacity can be agreed and the decision recorded in a way that would make it available in times of emergency.

If a valid advance decision to refuse medical treatment has been made (which is applicable to the decision needed in an MHA assessment) then that treatment cannot be given under the MCA (unless s26 applies). In such a case the use of the MHA can be considered, to provide treatment, if the MHA legal criteria are met. However:

- An advance decision opposed to ECT cannot be overridden by the MHA (except in an emergency under s62(1A)).
- Someone on a **community treatment order (CTO)** but currently in the community can also make an advance decision to refuse medical treatment, and this treatment could then only be provided if they are recalled to hospital.
- Where a patient has made a valid advance decision banning the use of a particular treatment option, but is otherwise agreeable to other forms of treatment, the assessing team should consider whether the use of formal powers are justified when other sorts of treatment are available and the patient does not object to accepting them (in which case they can be given informally with consent, or under the MCA if capacity is lacking).

Other things to remember about advance decisions:

- People with capacity can change their minds and change a previously made advance decision.

- If medication is given under the MHA in circumstances where an advance decision forbids it – unless the person regains capacity and agrees to the use of the treatment – the advance decision will become valid and applicable again as soon as the MHA detention ends, and the professionals involved with that person's care will be obliged to stop using the treatment or risk losing their protection from liability.

Example from practice

Janet has a diagnosis of paranoid delusional disorder that is managed with antipsychotic medication. About three months ago she stopped taking her medication and has become unwell as a result. Her father tells the AMHP that Janet has always maintained that she doesn't want to be put on depot medication, which she perceives to be 'demeaning'. Her key worker confirms this, describing a discussion with Janet when she had capacity, about her objection to the use of a depot. The AMHP is therefore satisfied that Janet has made a valid and applicable advance decision not to be treated with depot medication.

When assessed to decide if she needed to be detained, Janet is clearly very defensive and paranoid. Both doctors feel she does have a mental disorder of a nature or degree that warrants admission for assessment under s2. However, the consultant says that he plans to start Janet on depot medication. Janet becomes angry and agitated. She will come into hospital informally, stay there and take any medication she says, but not a depot. After consideration, the AMHP decides to respect her advance decision and not make an application, but provide Janet with the option of complying informally with other forms of treatment.

The AMHP is satisfied that she has sufficient capacity to agree to informal admission, has made a valid and applicable advance decision and that, as there is a less restrictive way of providing her with 'good enough' care, and such care would be in her best interests, this can be given, and professionals' interventions protected by s5 of the MCA if needed.

Lasting Powers of Attorney and deputies from the Court of Protection

People can plan in advance to give someone else the power to make decisions on their behalf, including decisions about whether or not to accept treatment for mental disorder. If the person themselves makes the arrangements while they still have capacity, the person is said to have given to a **donee** 'Lasting Power of Attorney'. If the Court of Protection makes the arrangements, the decision maker is a '**deputy** from the Court of Protection'.[9]

Because donees of LPAs and deputies can make a range of decisions, (including about admission and treatment) it is important to check whether they exist when setting up an MHA assessment.

The MHA and the MCA: making decisions about the care and treatment of people with mental health problems

Given the importance of working collaboratively with people wherever possible, and using the MHA as a last resort, the obvious place to start has to be working with people with their informed consent. If that isn't possible, the second option if the person lacks capacity could be working within the framework of the MCA. Finally, the option of using the MHA remains.

So a useful place to start in most cases has to be, 'why wouldn't the patient's own consent or the protections of the MCA be enough?' The MCA wouldn't be enough if:

- the person has capacity and refuses intervention;
- the person lacks capacity but needs assessment or treatment for a mental disorder, and they are objecting to receiving the care or treatment that they need;
- they have a valid and applicable advance decision or someone who has a relevant LPA and either of these is in conflict with an essential part of the care plan;
- it is not possible to give the person the care or treatment they need without doing something that is likely to deprive them of their liberty (such as admitting them onto a psychiatric ward);
- the person currently lacks capacity, and isn't objecting, but is expected to regain capacity and start to object, making ongoing treatment problematic (and there is not an alternative, less restrictive option);
- professionals feel they need the authority to specify where a person with a mental disorder should live, and someone with LPA is opposed to this suggestion;
- MCA powers are not available or appropriate;
- there is a significant risk to other people;
- it is important to have access to the MHA rights to appeal.

If any of the above issues are present in a case, you are more likely to need to use the authority of the Mental Health Act.

Working in human rights and equality rights compliant ways: the role of the Code of Practice

We now consider the legal status of the Mental Health Code of Practice and how the Guiding Principles should influence and support best practice.

i   The Code provides *statutory* guidance to **registered medical practitioners** ('doctors'), approved clinicians, managers and staff of hospitals, and approved mental health professionals on how they should proceed when undertaking duties under the Act. These professionals should have detailed knowledge of the Code, including its purpose, function and scope.

ii   It gives *statutory guidance* to registered medical practitioners and other professionals in relation to the medical treatment of patients suffering from mental disorder.

iii The guidance given in the Code to local authorities and their staff is statutory guidance given under s7 of the Local Authority and Social Services Act 1970. (duty to exercise social services functions under guidance of the Secretary of State).

iv   *The people listed above to whom to Code is addressed must have regard to the Code.* It is important that these persons have training on the Code and ensure that they are familiar with its requirements. As departures from the Code could give rise to legal challenge, reasons for any departure should be recorded clearly. Courts will scrutinise such reasons to ensure that there is sufficiently convincing justification in the circumstances.

CoP Introduction, p.12 (emphasis added, bold added)

The emphasis added above is important, because it highlights the legal obligation of professionals, and particularly AMHPs (who are approved by local authorities), to follow the advice of the Code, and if they (and other professionals) can't, to record why.

The Code also says that those who commission police, ambulance and health services are among those who should know the Code.

The MHA also specified that the Code should include principles that professionals are expected to use to influence their decision-making. The box below gives the wording for the principles attached to the English Code of Practice (in Wales there is a different Code and different principles).

Least restrictive option and maximising independence Where it is possible to treat a patient safely and lawfully without detaining them under the Act, the patient should not be detained. Wherever possible a patient's independence should be encouraged and supported with a focus on promoting recovery wherever possible.

Empowerment and involvement Patients should be fully involved in decisions about care, support and treatment. The views of families, carers and others, if appropriate, should be fully considered when taking decisions. Where decisions are taken which are contradictory to views expressed, professionals should explain the reasons for this.

Respect and dignity Patients, their families and carers should be treated with respect and dignity and listened to by professionals.

Purpose and effectiveness Decisions about care and treatment should be appropriate to the patient, with clear therapeutic aims, promote recovery and should be performed to current national guidelines and/or current, available best practice guidelines.

Efficiency and equity Providers, commissioners and other relevant organisations should work together to ensure that the quality of commissioning and provision of mental healthcare services are of high quality and are given equal priority to physical health and social care services. All relevant services should work together to facilitate timely, safe and supportive discharge from detention.

CoP, Guiding Principles, p.22

How the act, code and principles fit together

Quite simply, the Act tells us *what* to do; the Code explains *how* to do it; and the Guiding Principles help us to apply the Act in *individual situations*.

The notion is that the Principles are a framework of important values which help us focus on the best interest of the individual. The Principles make the practitioner consider the questions, 'Who?', 'How?' and 'Why?'.

Taking practical steps to help service users participate as fully as possible in the assessment process

Issues to consider include:

- Is there a time of the day when the patient is more alert or able to communicate? For example, anti-psychotic medication can make people drowsy. Finding a time when people feel more alert can be helpful.
- Where would the service user feel most comfortable?
- Is it possible to involve an advocate or family member? Would this be helpful?
- Are there cultural or gender issues to consider? Will the service user prefer to talk to men or women? Who can you ask as part of the information-gathering process?
- Will you need an interpreter?

To ensure you work respectfully with carers, friends and other family members, consider the following:

- Have you talked to everyone with relevant information?
- Have you listened to everyone's view, and acknowledged it, even in situations where you may disagree?
- Have you asked for help from the people who know the person best, so that you can understand the service user's 'world view', and discovered whether or how their viewpoints *differ* or are the same as those around them and people in a similar position or culture?

Of course, all these check points have to be considered in the context of the situation of the assessment. In some situations you may have these conversations while you are walking down the hallway into the patient's front room, chatting to their brother or sister as you go! However, don't forget they still need to be recorded.

Summary

- Always be clear about what you feel you need to do, why you need to do it and on whose authority you are relying when intervening.
- AMHPs and other professionals are expected to act and make decisions that are human rights and equality rights compliant – and as long as you follow the guidance of the Code of Practice and guidance following case law you are likely to be compliant.
- Remember you are expected to follow the advice of the Code of Practice unless you have a good reason not to. Even if you can't follow the advice of the MHA Code, you should still use the principles to influence your decisions, and record the decision and how you made it.
- Children and young people are also covered by the MHA, and you need to be clear about when it is okay to rely on parental authority, and when you should consider using the MHA.

Notes

1 P v Cheshire West and Chester Council and another and P and Q v Surrey County Council. 2014. WLR 2. https://www.supremecourt.uk/decided-cases/docs/UKSC_2012_0068_Judgment.pdf
2 This section on the Equality Act 2010 has been provided by Jo Honigmann of Just Equality.
3 Mental Capacity Act 2005: post-legislative scrutiny, Select Committee on the Mental Capacity Act 2005, Report of Session 2013-14: 13/3/2014
4 https://www.gov.uk/deprivation-of-liberty-orders
5 Re D (UK Supreme Court https://www.supremecourt.uk/cases/docs/uksc-2018-0064-judgment.pdf)
6 D(A Child; deprivation of liberty), Re [2015] EWHC 922 (Fam) (31 March 2015)
7 CoP 19.38-19.43
8 https://www.gov.uk/court-of-protection

2 Setting up Mental Health Act assessments

Organising the MHA assessment (MHAA) is a key task for AMHPs, and this chapter looks at the processes and issues that need to be considered.

By the end of the chapter, you should have an understanding of:

- When you should consider undertaking an MHA assessment
- What information you need to collect prior to the assessment
- How to make judgements about risk and urgency
- The legal powers in the MHA intended to ensure people are assessed – s5(2) and 5(4), s4, s136 and s135
- When to involve the police
- How to identify and consult with the right people
- When and how to delegate or displace the nearest relative
- Conflicts of interests in the assessing team, and maintaining independence
- How to work with advocates and interpreters in MHA assessments
- Thinking ahead about resources you may need for the assessment

Introduction

One of the confusions that often happens between mental health professionals, and people not so familiar with our services, comes up where people approach asking for help. Professionals from other disciplines may approach you saying 'so and so needs an MHA assessment' where in fact they need to have an assessment of their mental state; or family members may call saying that you must 'do' something, that they can't cope any more. In both cases, the first actions of the AMHP is to pick apart this request to gain a better understanding of what the person is really asking for, and to consider what might be most likely to help. It is also useful to establish why help is needed now, as this will enable you to start making judgements about how urgent the situation is (see Table 2.1).

Table 2.1 Useful questions

Question	Outcome
Does the referrer think the prospective patient needs to be compulsorily admitted to hospital, using force if necessary?	If yes, find out more about the risks and how urgent the situation is. Is it something that has to happen today or can it wait?
	If no, would the person agree to visiting their GP or A&E to get help? Have they called the local NHS mental health crisis line? Is there another service that may help?
Is the referrer the 'nearest relative' (NR) of the patient? (See pp. 51–54 for more information.)	If they are, they have a right to ask that an MHA assessment is considered, and if the AMHP decides not to apply for the person's admission, they must write to the nearest relative and let them know why assessment/admission is not appropriate.
Why has the request come in now?	Answers to this question will help you to gauge the urgency of the request.
Is anyone currently at risk?	Make sure you ask about any children the person has, especially if they care for them, as well as checking whether they care for adults for care and support needs. Be particularly careful of indications that the person may be suicidal, or experiencing delusional beliefs that incorporate people around them, as these situations may prove particularly risky.

Assessments in police custody

It is not uncommon to receive requests from colleagues in the police service asking for help with a person who has been arrested for an offence, whose presentation in custody is causing concern. The first source of assessment for people in custody is usually a forensic medical examiner (FME) or a specialist forensic nurse or social worker (depending on what has been commissioned locally). However, police may not have access to these resources, and requests may be more 'unfiltered'.

Whoever has seen the person first, and recommended a Mental Health Act assessment, it is worth asking about the nature of the offence the person has committed, and whether the police believe that it is likely that if admission to hospital (either formally or informally) is recommended by the team, the custody sergeant would be happy to bail the person to the hospital, so that they can receive the assessment and treatment they need.

As a rough 'rule of thumb', the more serious the offence (especially those involving risks to other people) the less likely it is that the police (and the CPS) will be willing to bail them.

If there is little chance that the person will be bailed, a full Mental Health Act assessment is unlikely to be appropriate, and more discussion about what is needed will be helpful. It may be that advice is needed on how to manage someone safely in custody, or what medication the person needs. Ultimately, where a person has committed a serious offence, it will be up to the Courts to ask for reports to help them understand how the person's mental health impacts on their offending, and what options are available to the courts in terms of what happens next.

Remember!

Section 13(1) requires AMHPS to 'consider' whether or not a Mental Health Act assessment should proceed – there isn't a 'requirement' that one should happen. It provides an opportunity for AMHPs to slow the process down, consider different views and options, and only move onwards with planning the actual assessment if that is the most appropriate thing to do.

When does an assessment start?

In some areas, MHA assessments are all handled by duty systems. In such cases, judging when a professional is moving from their 'substantive' role into that of an AMHP is fairly straightforward. They will be 'acting on behalf' of the local social service authority (LSSA) when they are 'on duty'.

However, in other cases, assessments are undertaken within teams and it can be harder to determine the start point. In practical terms, the following definition may be helpful:

A worker moves into an AMHP role and therefore starts to act 'on behalf of the local social services authority' (and needs to be covered by the LSSA's public liability insurance, access to legal advice, etc.) at the point where they are

either

- asked by their manager or a nearest relative to consider assessing someone under the MHA

or

- decide themselves they need to make a professional decision to involve doctors in an assessment *with a view to deciding whether an admission to hospital or other use of compulsion is necessary or proper.*

Example from practice

Alex (an AMHP) and Helen (a consultant psychiatrist) undertake a home visit to review Hera. In the past, it has been possible to treat Hera's bipolar disorder with extra medication in the community, as long as intervention is early. When Alex and Helen arrive at her home, it quickly becomes clear that things are worse than expected. Alex and Helen discuss with the Crisis Team whether they might be able to provide appropriate support, and a worker visits to set up a care plan. However, when the Crisis Team worker arrives, Hera becomes more agitated and starts to throw and break household items.

Alex decides that Hera would not cooperate with a home-based care plan. With Helen's agreement they decide to assess Hera under the MHA.

The MHA assessment, the local authority's responsibility for the process and their **vicarious liability** for Alex all begin when she decides to undertake the assessment.

Remember!

If someone needs to be reinterviewed because there was no bed available at the end of the initial assessment, and the AMHP who undertook the initial assessment is no longer available, the second AMHP must also interview the person themselves, and be satisfied that the criteria for admission are still met.

Gathering relevant information

Whether an assessment starts in an emergency situation, or in a more planned manner, the first task for the AMHP is to gather relevant information.

Checklist

Sources of information may include:
- ✓ family (including, but not exclusively, the NR)
- ✓ friends
- ✓ professionals involved with the person (psychiatrist, GP, care coordinator, district nurses, etc.)
- ✓ written information from past assessments (if relevant, risk assessments and case files)
- ✓ anyone holding a relevant lasting power of attorney for the person concerned

✓ any written information relating to advance decisions or statements
✓ information from the police (especially in community-based assessments where there may be unknown risk involved)
✓ information regarding issues of equality and diversity.

All information should be considered with regard to its *relevance* to the current situation, its *reliability* and any issues of the patient's or other people's *confidentiality*:

Relevance: This is an important question to ask about any information. What does the information provided (or requested) have to do with the current situation you are facing? If it is historical information, what makes it relevant to the issues you are currently dealing with?

Reliability: This relates not just to where the information comes from, but when. For example, a previous AMHP report naming a particular person as the NR a) may have been based on an incorrect choice, or b) may be affected by changed circumstances since the choice was made.

Confidentiality: You have a general professional responsibility to maintain clients' confidentiality. However, as the following 'golden rules'[1] of information sharing make clear, the Data Protection Act should not be used as a barrier for sharing necessary information:

The seven golden rules to sharing information

The following 'golden rules' have been taken directly from the following government guidance:

1 Remember that the General Data Protection Regulations (GDPR), Data Protection Act 1998 and human rights law are not barriers to justified information sharing, but provide a framework to ensure that personal information about living individuals is shared appropriately.
2 Be open and honest with the individual (and/or their family where appropriate) from the outset about why, what, how and with whom information will, or could, be shared, and seek their agreement, unless it is unsafe or inappropriate to do so.
3 Seek advice from other practitioners if you are in any doubt about sharing the information concerned, without disclosing the identity of the individual where possible.
4 Share with informed consent where appropriate and, where possible, respect the wishes of those who do not consent to share confidential information. Under the GDPR and Data Protection Act 1998, you may still share information without consent if, in your judgement, there is a lawful basis to do so, such as where safety may be at risk. You will need to base your judgment on the facts of the case. When you are sharing or requesting personal

information from someone, be certain of the basis upon which you are doing so. Where you have consent, be mindful that an individual might not expect information to be shared.

5 Consider safety and wellbeing: Base your information sharing decisions on considerations of the safety and wellbeing of the individual and others who may be affected by their actions.

6 Necessary, proportionate, relevant, adequate, accurate, timely and secure: Ensure that information you share is necessary for the purpose for which you are sharing it, is shared only with those individuals who need to have it, is accurate and up-to-date, is shared in a timely fashion, and is shared securely (see principles).

7 Keep a record of your decision and the reasons for it – whether it is to share information or not. If you decide to share, then record what you have shared, with whom and for what purpose.

Information sharing: key points

- While all professional groups have their own codes of confidentiality, confidentiality is relative to the risks of a particular situation.

- While it may not be possible to pass on information to someone about a person without their consent, there is nothing that stops you *listening* to what people need to tell you, be they neighbours, friends, etc. You can also ask for information in some circumstances, as long as you don't share information about the person inappropriately.

- If the person lacks capacity, it may be possible to consider exchanging information on the basis that to do so would be in their best interest.

- If the information you need is particularly important, it is worth asking the question, 'whose information is it?' For example, written information in case notes is often the property of the employing authority, not the person, so one possibility could be to approach an employer and ask them for relevant information.

- It is also worth asking 'why do I need this information?' If the need relates to risk to the person or others, it may be possible to argue that there is a 'public interest' in the information being disclosed to you. While patient confidentiality is important, the expectations on professionals to share relevant information is generally high. Numerous investigations have focused on problems around information sharing, and in risky situations it may be harder to justify *not* sharing information than it is to justify sharing it.

Judging risk and urgency

A lot of early work in an assessment hinges on deciding how urgent the situation is. Is this something that calls for immediate action, or can a more considered approach be taken?

Systemic risk assessment

One useful way of judging information is by using what is known as a **systemic risk assessment**. This can also be used later as part of the decision-making process, but is helpful to consider here. Asking about these issues in this way will not only help to clarify your own thinking about what to do and how quickly, but also help you to gain professional support from, for example, the police or ambulance services, as you will be able to be clear about what you need and why it is important to have it in the timescale you suggest. The important thing is to consider current risk behaviour in the context of past risk behaviour in order to really make effective assessments of risk.

In systemic risk assessment, the following issues are considered:

- **Recency** How recent is the risk behaviour you are concerned about? This may include delusional beliefs that affect the patient's functioning as well as risk to safety of others. The more recent it is, the more relevant it often is.
- **Frequency** This refers to the frequency of the occurrence of the risk behaviour over the patient's mental health history, not just currently. However, an increased frequency of risk behaviour often indicates an increasing urgency.
- **Severity** How serious or severe is the risk behaviour? How serious has it been in the past? Have weapons been involved and how have they been used? You need to consider both the severity of risk to the individual service user as well as to others. When increased frequency is matched by increased severity, this is of particular concern.
- **Pattern** Sometimes this is referred to as the 'context' of the risk behaviour, and it is essential to your overall judgement. Where there is a clearly documented pattern of risk behaviour, by considering the context in which the risk behaviour previously occurred, you will have some indication of the level of concern you should be feeling. For example, someone who, while unwell, experiences delusions about women but feels safe with men will present more risk in a mixed-gender environment (like a ward) than in a male-only environment (like a prison).
- **Prominence of thinking** Where delusional or destructive ideas are evident, how much impact do they have on the person concerned? For example, are they able to resist thoughts of harming themselves or others?
- **Effect** What would be the consequence of the risk behaviour should it occur? Who would it affect? Who might need to be protected? It is not only risk behaviour; risk beliefs also need to be considered. What is the effect of the beliefs on the life of the service user, their support systems, their social functioning as well as risk to self or others? Are there children or other vulnerable adults in the house who may need protection in their own right?

Risk management and children

The National Inquiry into Homicides and Suicides found that there were particular issues associated with the deaths of children by parents with mental health problems. These were:

- where the parent/carer had a delusional disorder, and the children had become involved in their delusional beliefs;
- where as a consequence of divorce or separation, one partner became depressed or suicidal and took their own and the children's lives.

Where you find these issues are apparent, particular care should be taken, and a Mental Health Act assessment should be considered whenever the adult concerned is unwilling to seek help informally.

Have all alternatives to an MHA assessment been considered?

Although alternatives to the use of **compulsion** must be considered as part of the assessment, it is also worth considering whether there are alternatives available *before* starting the formal MHA assessment process – unless you have to assess because, for example, the person is in a place of safety on an s136.

Using Crisis Resolution or Home Treatment teams[2]

Risk assessment prior to organising an MHA assessment will also help to determine whether it is appropriate to use a crisis resolution or home treatment approach, rather than focusing solely on setting up an MHA.

Crisis resolution/home treatment (CRHT) teams generally act as 'gate keepers' for admission to hospital, i.e. everyone considered for admission to hospital should also be referred to the CRHT. The principle is that an alternative to admission should at least be considered for everyone. This ties in with the AMHP's obligation to consider the least restrictive option.

Many users and carers prefer community-based treatment as it allows people to stay in a familiar social and cultural environment. The CRHT model is based on working with individual service users' needs and strengths. Home treatment has to be negotiated and agreed between the user and team.

> ### Remember!
>
> AMHPs have 14 days after the signing of the second medical recommendation to decide whether or not to apply for the service user to be detained in hospital. This time could be used to 'trial' the use of crisis team support.

Planned MHA assessments will often have been discussed with the CRHT prior to the assessment. A joint assessment may have already taken place to consider if CRHT involvement would be possible. It is always helpful to ask the CRHT to attend an MHA assessment in the community where they have not previously been involved with a service user unless there are clear reasons not to do so; for example there are known serious risks which would make CRHT an inappropriate response.

As well as being involved in community assessments where admission to hospital is being considered, CRHT involvement can also be used to support an inpatient return home more quickly.

The decision about whether to use a CRHT approach or an admission approach will be influenced by many factors. Table 2.2 gives some pointers to

Table 2.2   Responding to a crisis situation

Pointers towards admission to hospital	Pointers towards community-based care with crisis team/home treatment team intervention
Accommodation instability	Settled/safe accommodation – although CRHTs can work with people in a variety of accommodation or who are able to stay with family/friends who are supportive
Risk to self or others which requires active management/containment	
Client unwilling/unable to negotiate about care and treatment at home, including access	Client/carer is able to negotiate and agree about interventions and care, including access
Carers or other significant others not coping or difficult family dynamics (Crisis House consideration if available)	Client is able to negotiate about risks to self
	Other risks are not so acute that containment in hospital is necessary
Active substance misuse and where this is the primary issue (detox)	Supportive family/friends – although not necessarily
Previous failed recent CRHT intervention	Previous positive use of CRHT intervention
	Client/carer able/willing to contact the team if needed
Client finds it hard to cope with seeing different people, or needing to wait in to see team members	Client able to cope with seeing different people and at different times
Client very distressed by symptoms or feels too unsafe	Client is known to community mental health team (CMHT) or CRHT
Concerns over serious physical health issues	Cultural or social factors that would make home treatment preferable
Out of hours it may be more difficult to establish information and support available	Within hours it may be possible to establish information and involve care coordinators, etc.

consider when working with the CRHT members to decide how best to respond to a crisis situation.

Where a patient is already detained under an s135, s136 or s5(2), an MHA assessment will almost always be needed – but it may still be appropriate to involve the CRHT with the assessment to ensure that all alternatives to admission are considered. In other situations, it may be more appropriate to involve the team first, before asking for an MHA assessment. For example, where a known patient is going into crisis, but does not yet need compulsory admission to hospital.

Setting up MHA assessments in different situations

There are two main types of situation where an MHA assessment will be carried out:

1 where the patient is already a hospital inpatient, and is unwilling to accept assessment or treatment and the use of s5/2 or 5/4 is justified to ensure an MHA assessment takes place;
2 where the patient is in the community, is unwilling to accept necessary assessment or treatment informally, and the use of s135, s136 or s4 is justified.

Of course, there are situations both in the community and for hospital inpatients, where it is possible to set up a Mental Health Act Assessment without the use of formal powers (for example, where a patient is happy to wait in hospital until an MHA assessment can be arranged, or where a husband or wife can provide access to a patient in their home, to allow an assessment to be set up) and if it possible to do so, then assessments should be set up 'informally.'

Remember!

As a general rule, the decision about whether a patient on s2 should be referred for an assessment for s3 should be made at least a week before the end of the s2, to ensure that there is enough time for AMHPs to contact, and usefully consult, the nearest relative. However, if the nearest relative objected to the use of s2, and is likely to object to the use of s3, extra effort should be made to maintain contact with the nearest relative from the point of admission under s2. This would help to ensure that the nearest relative's (NR's) views can be fully taken into account, and the concerns of the clinical team discussed with them early in case the AMHP needs to consider going to court for a displacement order.

Characteristics of sections that last 72 hours or less

Where someone isn't willing to comply with an MHA assessment informally, the powers available include s135, 136, s5(2/4) and s4 exist, and all share the same characteristics, but timescales may vary:

- Sections that apply where someone is already an inpatient (s5/4, or s5/2) last for up to 72 hours (s5(4) lasts for 6 hours but can be extended for up to 72 hours following an assessment by a doctor).
- Sections that apply where someone is in the community, and where police support is involved (s135 and s136) last for 24 hours, but can be extended for a further 12 hours in certain circumstances.
- They all provide the authority to detain a person in a particular place to allow a full MHA assessment to happen.
- None of the sections confer any authority to treat the person against their will – so if medication is needed while people are waiting to be assessed, this must either be provided on the basis that the person agrees, or on the basis that they lack capacity to make that particular decision, and it would be in their best interests to receive the treatment being suggested.
- The patient has no right of appeal during the period of detention (although with s4, the person may lodge an appeal within the 72 hours, which will be submitted to the MHRT service if the second doctor agrees that admission under s2 is appropriate).
- They have no right of access to an IMHA (an Independent Mental Health Advocate) but do have rights to information.
- These sections cannot be renewed – if the patient has not been seen within the allotted time, they are free to leave the hospital unless they are willing to remain informally (see below).

Managing situations where the authority to detain has expired or does not exist

Some of the most difficult situations to manage occur in A&Es, or **Health-based places of Safety (HBPoS)** where the authority to detain under s135/6 is about to expire, the person clearly needs to be detained, but no bed is available; or where someone presents informally at A&E, is clearly very unwell, but isn't willing to stay until an assessment can take place, or a bed can be located. There is no completely right answer, but here are some points to consider:

- If the s135/6 authority to detain has not been extended, could it be? (See p.41.)
- If the person attended A&E informally, might the police be willing to use their powers under s136 to make them stay?

- If the person has presented informally, and there will be a long wait for a bed, or for the right person to be available to conduct the assessment (because, for example, a Child and Adolescent Mental Health Service – CAMHS – doctor is needed) is it possible to admit the person to an inpatient ward, where s5/2 could be used if the person wanted to leave?
- All areas are expected to have an s140 policy, which should specify where in cases of 'special urgency' a person could be admitted to. In some areas, trusts have decided to 're designate' their HBPoS under s140, to allow the person to be admitted there. This is possible where the HBPoS is within the grounds of the psychiatric hospital.
- If the person clearly lacks capacity to decide on staying, the MCA provides some short term protection for those feeling they need to stop a person leaving in their best interests.

Finally, where all options have been exhausted (i.e. you have no legal framework available) what's left is our obligation to work in ways which protect people's fundamental human rights – in this case the right to life (Article 1) and being able to argue that the risks someone poses to themselves or others is so high and so immediate, that there was no other option but to prevent them leaving, even if this meant depriving them of their right to liberty (Article 5).

In all cases, make contemporaneous notes of why you are making the decisions you feel are needed, escalate and record the case as a high-risk incident.

Short-term sections in detail

Section 5(4) (CoP chapter 18)

Whose power? Nurses who are registered by the Nursing and Midwifery Council in sub-parts 1 or 2 as specialists in mental health or learning disabilities.

What is the power? This provides the authority for nurses to prevent an informal patient (i.e. someone who has already been admitted onto a ward) from leaving the ward for up to 6 hours. (This power should be used when it isn't possible for a doctor/**approved clinician (AC)** to see the patient immediately.)

What are the criteria? It should be used where it is immediately necessary to prevent a patient leaving hospital, before a doctor can arrive to assess them. The nurse (whose individual decision the use of the section is) must be satisfied that the person has a mental disorder whose symptoms are currently so acute that there would be a risk to the patient's health or safety, or the safety of other people, if they were to leave the hospital.

When does the authority start? It starts as soon as the nurse completes the necessary form. The nurse should also record the reasons for using the s5(4) in the notes. The patient must be on the hospital grounds at the time the papers are signed for the power to be effective. The completed H2 form must be sent to the hospital managers (usually via the MHA administrator).

When does it end? The authority ends as soon as the doctor or AC sees and assesses the patient. If they agree an MHA assessment is needed (see below), the length of the section will be extended to the full 72 hours from the time of the nurse's recording of the s5(4) detention.

Other issues to consider:

- How soon before a doctor or an approved clinician can get to the ward?
- What is the potential risk to the patient and others if the patient leaves immediately?

Nurses should particularly consider:

- the patient's expressed intentions
- the likelihood of the patient harming themselves or others
- the likelihood of the patient behaving violently
- any evidence of disordered thinking
- the patient's current behaviour and, in particular, any changes in their usual behaviour
- the patient's recent communication with relatives and friends
- whether the date is one of special significance for the patient (e.g. the anniversary of a bereavement)
- any recent disturbances on the ward
- any relevant involvement of other patients
- any history of unpredictability or impulsiveness
- any formal risk assessments which have been undertaken (specifically looking at previous behaviour), and
- any other relevant information from other members of the multi-disciplinary team.

CoP 18:30

Section 5(2) (CoP chapter 18)

Whose power? This power can be exercised by the doctor or AC in charge of the patient's treatment or their nominated deputy. Only the doctor or AC in charge of the patient's treatment can nominate a deputy – and only one deputy for a patient may be nominated at any one time. It is unlawful for one deputy to nominate another (CoP 18.13). However, a job role can be nominated rather than a named person (such as the junior doctor for a ward) but the person nominated must be competent, and if they are not themselves an AC or s12 doctor, they should be supported in decision-making about using s5(2) by someone who is (CoP 18.14).

The patient must be an inpatient but need not be in hospital for treatment of a mental disorder. Therefore the doctor in charge of treatment of a patient in an acute hospital may also use an s5(2) to prevent the patient leaving, where they believe the patient has a mental disorder and needs assessment for admission to hospital for that disorder.

What is the power? This section allows the doctor or AC to prevent the patient leaving for up to 72 hours, in order that an MHA assessment can be undertaken.

What are the criteria? It should be used when it appears to the doctor/AC in charge of a patient's treatment, or their nominated deputy, that an informally admitted patient needs to be formally detained under the MHA. In effect, the doctor/AC is saying that they believe that the person meets the criteria for s2 or s3 of the Act, namely:

- They have a mental disorder of a nature or degree that warrants formal admission to hospital.
- There would be a risk to the health or safety of the patient, or the safety of other people, if they were not detained.
- There isn't a reasonable alternative to that detention.

When does it start? If the patient was on an s5(4) prior to the start of the assessment, the 72 hours will start from the beginning of that section. In other cases, the 72 hours will start once the s5(2) paperwork is 'delivered' to the hospital managers. (This might be by hand, or via the internal mail system for example.)

When does it end? The s5(2) ends either when a decision is made by the AC or doctor that an MHA assessment is not needed, or when an assessment under the MHA has been completed and a decision to admit or not has been reached.

Other issues to consider:

- The use of s5(2) is an individual decision, so it is not appropriate for a more senior doctor or AC to leave an instruction for their deputy to use an s5(2) if the patient tries to leave (for example).
- It isn't possible to transfer someone who is 'held' on s5 to another hospital unless either a) the person agrees or b) the risks in the case are such that use of s4 can be justified or c) they lack capacity for the decision and the move would be in their best interest (CoP 18.42-45). If after transfer the person tries to leave the new hospital, the Code (18:44) suggests this should be seen as a new situation, and the receiving hospital should consider using its own 5/2.
- The power can only be used for an informally admitted patient, who you have personally seen. It cannot be used in A&E for example, or outpatients.

There is no power to enforce treatment while on s5/2. If treatment is needed, it must be provided either with the consent of the person, or using the MCA if they lack capacity.

Section 4 – emergency admission

Whose power? This section requires the agreement of an AMHP and a doctor. That doctor need not be s12 approved.

What is the power? This power should be used in emergency situations (which may include police stations and A&E departments), where the risks posed by the patient are such that it isn't possible to wait for the arrival of a second doctor. The powers include:

- the power to convey the patient to hospital (by force if necessary), which lasts for up to 24 hours from being seen by the doctor;
- the power to detain the patient in hospital for up to 72 hours, and the 72 hours starts from the time the patient arrives at the hospital.

There is no power to enforce treatment (as mentioned above) and no right to appeal (although an appeal can be lodged and will be dealt with if the second doctor agrees that the patient does need to be detained under s2).

What are the criteria? Section 4 should be used when it is of urgent necessity to detain the patient under s2 and waiting for a second doctor to complete such an assessment would involve undesirable delay. In other words:

- The person would meet the criteria for s2.
- They have a mental disorder of a nature or degree that warrants admission for assessment or assessment followed by treatment for at least a limited period.
- There would be risks to their health or safety, or the safety of other people if they were not admitted.
- There is not a reasonable alternative to formal admission.

And there is evidence to support the view that you could not reasonably be expected to wait for a second doctor because, for example:

- There would be an immediate and significant risk of mental or physical harm to the patient or to others
- A danger of serious harm to property or
- A need for the use of restrictive interventions on the patient (see CoP chapter 26)

CoP 15.8

When does it start? The authority to convey starts as soon as the AMHP and doctor have completed their recommendation and application. The authority to detain and the 72-hour period starts from the point when the patient is admitted to the hospital. The nurse receiving the papers should record the time the patient arrived on form H3.

When does it end? The power of s4 ends either when a second doctor has completed their assessment and decided whether or not to provide a second recommendation for s2, or after 72 hours. It cannot be renewed. If the doctor agrees that it is appropriate to make a second medical recommendation for s2, the s2 will be deemed to have started when the person was first admitted on s4.

Remember!

If the patient was admitted on Monday 1 February on an s4 but not seen by a second doctor until Tuesday 2 February, the s2 would still run from the time on Monday when they were first admitted for 28 days.

Other issues to consider:

- If the first doctor was not s12 approved, the second doctor must be.
- If the patient is not seen by the second doctor within 72 hours, it would be inappropriate to use an s5(2) to detain them further. Another s4 order cannot be used and the patient would be free to leave.
- An s4 should only be used in cases of genuine emergency, not for the convenience of staff.
- It is possible to detain a patient who was admitted on s4 on an s3 rather than an s2, but in that case two new recommendations for s3 plus an application from an AMHP would also be needed.

Using the most appropriate place of safety

3.1 The legislation continues to provide for a range of locations to be used as a place of safety, which allows for local flexibility to respond to different situations. A person in mental health crisis should be taken to or kept at a place of safety that best meets their needs.

> Guidance for the implementation of
> changes to police powers and places of safety
> provisions in the Mental Health Act 1983

Section 136 – detaining a mentally disordered person anywhere that isn't someone's home

The guidance on the use of s135/6 can be found in 'Guidance for the implementation of changes to police powers and places of safety provisions in the mental health act 1983' published in October 2016.

Remember!

The 'Right Care Right Person' policy does not change the legal responsibilities the police have in relation to s135 and s136. However, it does make it more important to be clear about the risks you are concerned about, and be able in an emergency to articulate why the person or others are at such imminent risk that police need to be involved whether or not a warrant has been obtained.

Guidance for the implementation of
changes to police powers and places of safety
provisions 1.4/1.5

Whose power? This power can be used by a police constable. The constable should (if practical) take advice from mental health professionals on whether to use it, but the final decision remains with the individual police office.

What is the power? It is to take a person located in any place which is not a private residence, (or buildings or gardens associated with that residence) to a place of safety to allow an assessment of their mental health to take place.

What are the criteria? This section can be used when a police constable finds a person in a place that is not a private dwelling who appears to them to have a mental disorder, and to be in immediate need of care *or* control:

136(1A) states that the power under section 136(1) may be exercised where the person is in any place other than:

'(a) any house, flat or room where that person, or any other person, is living, or (b) any yard, garden, garage or outhouse that is used in connection with the house, flat or room, other than one that is also used in connection with one or more other houses flats or rooms.'

Guidance for the implementation of
changes to police powers and places of safety
s2.4

This definition means that an s136 can be used in a wide range of places, as long as the place isn't where someone is living. So police stations, A&E, communal hallways, railway sidings, roofs and places you would normally have to pay an entrance fee to enter all fall within the remit of s136.

This criteria –*'is in immediate need of care or control'* – covers two issues: that the need must be 'immediate' and that the person appears to be in need of 'care *or* control'. In practice, s136 is probably used more with a person who appears to be needing 'control' rather than someone who needs care. It is important to understand that either need is valid.

Consulting before using s136(1): Police are now obliged to consult MH services 'where it is practicable to do so, before deciding whether or not to keep a person at, or remove a person to, a place of safety under section 136(1)'.

The professionals they should consult include an AMHP, nurse, Dr, OT or paramedic. The purpose of the consultation is to help the PC decide whether it's appropriate to use the powers. In the box below are the issues the guidance suggests should be considered.

When does it start? The 24 hours start at the following points:

- from the point when the person arrives at the 'place of safety', or
- if they are already in a 'place of safety', when the decision is made to keep the person there, or
- if there is agreement to undertake the assessment in the place named in the warrant, the time starts from the moment the officer first entered the property.

2.11 The police officer should seek to ascertain, and the healthcare professional being consulted should offer, where possible, information or advice regarding:

- an opinion on whether this appears to be a mental health issue based on professional observation and, if possible, questioning of the person;
- whether other physical health issues may be of concern or contributing to behaviour (e.g. substance misuse, signs of physical injury or illness);
- whether the person is known to local health service providers;
- if so, whether it is possible to access medical records or any care plan to determine medical history and suggested strategies for appropriately managing a mental health crisis;
- whether in the circumstances, the proposed use of section 136 powers is appropriate;
- where it is determined that use of section 136 powers is appropriate – identification of a suitable health based place of safety, and facilitation of access to it;
- where it is determined that use of section 136 powers is not appropriate – identification and implementation of alternative arrangements (such as escorting the person home, to their own doctor, to hospital, or to a community place of calm/respite).

2.12 The police officer retains ultimate responsibility for the decision to use their section 136(1) powers, having considered the advice given to them as part of any consultation. The police officer should ensure that any consultation is recorded – including who was consulted and the advice they gave.

> Guidance for the implementation of
> changes to police powers and places of safety
> s2.11–2.12

What 'counts' as a 'place of safety'? Local policy should identify a place of safety to which people should be taken. In most cases this will be an A&E department, or a specialist s136 suite attached to a mental health unit. However, in law a 'place of safety' can be anywhere willing and able to take the patient on a temporary basis.

A place of safety is now defined in the Act as:-

* a hospital;
* an independent hospital or care home for mentally disordered persons;
* a police station;
* residential accommodation provided by a local social services authority;
* any other suitable place (with the consent of a person managing or residing at that place).

Guidance p12

Police stations cannot be used as a place of safety for someone aged under 18 years, and for adults can only be used where

(i)   the behaviour of the person poses an imminent risk of serious injury or death to themselves or another person;

(ii) because of that risk, no other place of safety in the relevant police area can reasonably be expected to detain them, and

(iii) so far as reasonably practicable, a healthcare professional will be present at the police station and available to them

The Mental Health Act 1983 (Places of Safety) Regulations 2017

If there is concern about a patient's physical health, they should be taken to A&E first.

Remember!

As a 'hospital' is by definition a place of safety, the 24 hours will start when the person arrives there (i.e. A&E) even if they are later transferred to a different place of safety (such as a health-based place of safety (HBPoS)).

Searching the person held under s136: There is now an explicit power under s136(C), allowing a constable to search someone held under s135 or s136, if they have a 'reasonable concern' that the person may have concealed something with which they may harm themselves or others. Officers can ask someone to remove outer clothes in order to conduct their search, but (beyond looking into someone's mouth) it does not allow a more 'intimate' search.

The purpose of removal under s136: MHA s136(2) is 'for the purpose of enabling him to be examined by a registered medical practitioner and to be interviewed by an AMHP and of making any necessary arrangements for his treatment or care'.

In other words, there are three expectations under s136.

- that a doctor examine the person;
- that an AMHP interview the person;
- that necessary arrangements are put in place for treatment or care.

The power to hold someone under s136 can end after the doctor's assessment, if they decide that the person doesn't have a mental disorder within the meaning of the MHA (for example, because their behaviour is caused only by the use of drugs or alcohol, with no other underlying mental disorder). In this case the s136 must end immediately and the person will be free to go. Alternatively, once the patient has been examined by an AMHP and doctor, the s136 will end once a decision has been made about what should happen next, and the 'necessary arrangements' are in place.

The possible 'arrangements' include:

1 informal admission;
2 formal detention under the MHA;
3 setting up an alternative support plan in the community;
4 the use of DoLS or guardianship to support a care plan.

This also means that the s136 can stay in place, and the person be held, until the 'necessary arrangements' – including finding a bed – are in place.

Extending the power to detain: The 24-hour period can be extended for an additional 12 hours, if in the view of the responsible doctor, because of the person's mental or physical presentation, it would be unrealistic to complete the assessment within 24 hours.

Transfers between places of safety: It is possible to transfer the patient between places of safety, provided it is in the best interests of the patient to do so.

The decision to transfer should be supported by a doctor or AMHP or other competent healthcare professional. The patient may be conveyed by an AMHP, police officer or anyone authorised by them. The patient may be conveyed more than once, if need be, within the 24–36-hour period

> ### Example from practice
>
> Kelly was picked up on an s136 one evening after police were called because she was 'behaving oddly'. When the first doctor saw her at the place of safety, he realised that she was known to the Assertive Outreach Team in an adjacent area, and was on a CTO. After discussion with the duty AMHP, they decided it would be more appropriate to use the s136 to transfer Kelly to the catchment ward for her team, so that she could be assessed by her own **responsible clinician** (RC) and professionals who knew her on following morning.

Other issues to consider:

- If a patient does have a mental disorder, even if they agree to a treatment plan when first seen by a doctor, they should still be interviewed by an AMHP to confirm the arrangements for that plan.
- If a more junior doctor makes the first assessment, they should discuss and confirm their decision with a more experienced colleague. The reasons why a s12 doctor was not involved at that point should be recorded in the notes.
- If the person being assessed has particular needs (for example, they have a learning disability, or are a young person) it is preferable to use assessors who have experience of that specialism.
- The initial assessor *and* the AMHP should enquire about the patient's home situation, for example finding out if there are dependent children, adults or pets who need to be taken care of as well as the patient themselves.
- The same standards should apply to assessments for s136 as applied to any other MHA assessment. So interpreters, for example, should be used as soon as reasonably possible.

> Assessment by the doctor and AMHP should begin as soon as possible after the arrival of the individual at the place of safety. In cases where there are no clinical grounds to delay assessment, it is good practice for the doctor and AMHP to attend within three hours; this is in accordance with best practice recommendations made by the Royal College of Psychiatrists. Where possible, the assessment should be undertaken jointly by the doctor and the AMHP.
>
> CoP 16:47

Setting up an MHA assessment in the community and the use of s135

Mental Health Act assessments may occur on private premises with or without police support. This part of the book looks at situations where the use of section 135 is required.

What the Act says: 'the justice may issue a warrant authorising any constable...to enter, if need be by force any premises specified in the warrant in which that person is believed to be, and, if thought fit, to remove him to a place of safety with a view to the making of an application...'

MHA S135(1)

Places where a s135 warrant may be needed:
When s135 and s136 were amended in 2017/18, Parliament changed the definition of where the two sections should be used. In effect, the law now defines in s136 when its powers can be used (anywhere *except* a house, flat or room where someone is living), and in doing so gives us a definition of where s135 is needed, which is below.

S136(1A)The power of a constable under subsection (1) may be exercised where the mentally disordered person is at any place, other than—

(a) any house, flat or room where that person, or any other person, is living, or

(b) any yard, garden, garage or outhouse that is used in connection with the house, flat or room, other than one that is also used in connection with one or more other houses, flats or rooms.

The great thing about this is it makes it clear that police can *either* use s136 *or* s135 depending on the circumstances if they need the authority to intervene in someone's life.

In most cases, this definition will be easy to apply. It will be clear whether you are looking at 'a place' where someone is living (or its associated land or building). If you are looking at a communal area (a hallway or a garden) you won't need an s135 warrant, and s136 would be available , but there are some areas where there are still debates.

Example from practice

Patric is living in a tent on a roundabout. He is behaving bizarrely and believes that the world is about to end and only he can save it. His mother asks local AMHPs to undertake an assessment. When the AMHPs approach the Court, they refuse to grant an s135 because they say a tent isn't somewhere people live. The local police are very unhappy about being asked to use powers under s136 because they say Patric is living there. While these arguments were happening, Patric was found walking naked through a local shopping centre, put on s136 and subsequently detained on s2. Local police and AMHP leads agreed to meet with magistrates to resolve this difference of opinion, and took legal representatives with them to help with legal interpretation.

So do you always need to use an s135 warrant when assessing in someone's home? Assessments on private premises with police support may occur with or without a warrant issued under s135(1) MHA, however the legal advice many police forces work to is that s135 should be sought where possible, as without it they have no authority to stay in the property if the householder requests that they leave. Therefore if you can't, or don't, feel that an s135 warrant can be obtained, be ready to be clear about why.

In all cases, preplanning the assessment is essential.

Where the police attend, they are responsible for controlling the operation for the purposes of entry into the premises and for ensuring the mitigation of identified risks.

Whenever you are conducting a community-based MHA assessment, you should consider whether the support of the police will be necessary, either to keep the assessing team safe or to ensure that you are able to successfully complete the assessment.

Remember!

Even if you have access to a key, unless you have permission from at least one of the home owners you will still need a warrant to legally gain access to the property.

When to consider applying to a magistrate for a warrant under s135(1)

You should consider applying for a warrant under s135 under the following circumstances:

- The risk assessment indicates a significant risk of harm either to the patient, the family, the assessing team or others.
- Based on current or past history it is likely that the patient will either refuse to admit you or may ask you to leave prior to the conclusion of the assessment.
- There isn't anyone except the patient who can provide you with the legal authority to be on the premises and conduct the assessment, and they are refusing or likely to start refusing.
- A relative has a key, but the patient is not willing to allow you access.

The warrant doesn't require you to know the name of the person involved, although clearly this is preferable, but you do need to be able to evidence why you believe the patient has a mental disorder, and why you believe they need assessment of their mental disorder.

> # Remember!
>
> The wording of an s135(1) does not require that you should have tried to see the patient already and been refused entry, but magistrates are likely to want to know why a warrant is needed, and if a visit has not already been attempted, you will be expected to demonstrate why not.

The statutory criteria in detail are shown in Table 2.3.

What power does the s135(1) warrant provide?

The warrant must be executed by a police officer, and there must be an AMHP and at least one doctor in attendance. The warrant provides the authority to enter (if necessary by force) the place where the person in the warrant is believed to be living and, if thought fit, remove them to a place of safety with either a view to making an application for their admission under the Act or making other arrangements for his treatment or care.

Table 2.3 The statutory criteria in detail

Criteria	Practical meaning
There is reasonable cause to suspect that a person is believed to be suffering from a mental disorder	That you have observed or have other reliable evidence indicating that a particular person is suffering from a mental disorder
Either s135(1)(a)	
That he has been, or is being, ill-treated, neglected or kept otherwise than under proper control	That the person concerned is living with others who are unable or unwilling to ensure that they receive the assessment or treatment that they need for his mental disorder (i.e. they are *neglecting* their need for assessment or treatment), or that they are ill-treating them
In any place within the jurisdiction of the magistrate	That you know where the person is, and their address is within the geographical area of this particular Justice of the Peace
Or s135(1)(b)	
Being unable to care for himself, is living alone in such a place	That the person is living alone, and isn't caring for themselves – including taking appropriate actions to allow assessment of their mental disorder, or take medication as prescribed

In other words, the decision about whether or not to detain the patient may be made either on the premises, (if the person living in the place is willing for the assessment to take place there) or at a place of safety (which could be the ward to which the patient is due to be admitted – with the agreement of that place).

If there is agreement that the assessment can continue in the person's home, legally the home will become a 'place of safety', and the 24-hour period during which the assessment must be completed will start from the time police first entered the property.

Reasons for removing someone to a place of safety could include:

- that it is inappropriate to complete the assessment in the community because of risks in the property (weapons, other people, etc.);
- that the person being assessed cannot properly be interviewed in a suitable manner while in the property, perhaps because it becomes clear that an interpreter is needed to complete the assessment;
- that the person (or someone else at the property) is either objecting to the assessment being completed in the premises (so you do not have agreement to stay) or unwilling or unable to provide agreement for the assessment to be completed there;
- that you want to make 'other arrangements for his treatment or care' such as removing them to a hospital ward for physical health care treatment or to a registered care home in order to make the arrangements for them to stay there using guardianship or a DoLS order.

Gaining 'agreement' to the use of a private dwelling as a place of safety
The wording of the law talks about gaining the 'agreement' of people to conduct an assessment in someone's home – so importantly while assessing capacity to make this decision would be good practice, it isn't explicitly required.

Pragmatically, professionals may want to focus on being satisfied that there *isn't an objection* to the person being assessed in a private dwelling, as much as being happy that those involved 'agree' to the assessment continuing.

When thinking about whose agreement is needed, Table 2.3 (below) from the guidance will be helpful.

Being satisfied that the person believed to be suffering from a mental disorder is able to agree to use of a private dwelling as a place of safety may in some circumstances be difficult. However mental ill health issues take a wide range of forms, and while a person may appear to be suffering from a mental disorder this does not necessarily mean that (s)he is unable to agree to use of a place as a place of safety. It will be relevant whether the person can understand the information relevant to the decision, retain that information, use or weigh that information as part of the process of making the decision, and communicate that decision.

S3.9 Guidance for the implementation of
changes to police powers and places of safety

Table 2.4

Scenario	Agreement required that person agrees to the use of the place as a place of safety
If the person believed to be suffering from a mental disorder is the sole occupier of the place	That person agrees to the use of the place as a place of safety
If the person believed to be suffering from a mental disorder is an occupier of the place but not the sole occupier	Both that person and one of the other occupiers agree to the use of the place as a place of safety
If the person believed to be suffering from a mental disorder is not an occupier of the place	Both that person and the occupier (or, if more than one, one of the occupiers) agree to the use of the place as a place of safety

Processes for obtaining s135 warrants

In most areas obtaining warrants from Magistrates Courts transferred to an online process during Covid, and this has continued. In many cases, these processes are efficient and provide a warrant within 24 hours. However, not all courts are as efficient, and if that is the case locally it is important to evidence problems, and escalate concerns to AMHP leads.

Situations where it isn't possible to obtain 'agreement' to assessing in the home

Because of the requirement to obtain 'agreement' prior to using these powers the implementation guide suggests that 'If they [the person] are clearly unable to understand or communicate with police or mental health professionals, the necessary agreement cannot be sought or obtained' (Police Implementation Guide s3.9).

The role of the police when undertaking assessments under s135

Police officers are obviously the people who will need to gain entry to the property (using force if needed) but they are also the people who have an overall responsibility for the safety of people and the environment, and for making sure people in the property understand what agreement means, and do give it freely.

Where another place is being used (say, a day centre or a room in a supermarket), the officers at the scene should seek the agreement of the most senior manager available, in order to use the place as a place of safety.

Remember!

A warrant can only be used once. Once it has been 'executed' (i.e. used to gain entry) it cannot be used again. If you force entry and the person isn't in, you will need to get a new warrant. In addition, a copy of the warrant should be left on the premises to confirm that it was used to gain entry to the property (even is no one was in).

Table 2.5 Summary and time line for s135 assessment

Timeline	Action
Pre-assessment planning	• Determine why an assessment using the police is needed, rather than a less 'authoritarian' approach (for example, assertively engaging the person via a crisis resolution approach)
	• Check that you have sufficient evidence to justify applying for a s135 warrant. If you haven't been able to see the person, why not?
	• Check what risks exist in terms of how and where the assessment should take place. Is there evidence that it would be dangerous for professionals or others to assess in the home?
	• Check whether the person is likely to be able to agree where the assessment should take place
	• If you are likely to remove the person to complete the assessment, where might they be taken? Should this be a ward, the health-based place of safety or elsewhere? Who would need to give agreement to using the proposed assessment location as a place of safety?
	• Check which doctors will be available to accompany you
	• Complete any necessary risk assessment, and discuss the assessment with the police
	• Consider the current bed situation, make arrangement as appropriate to ensure bed-managers/others are aware of the possibility of admission, and whether they can tell you where/when a bed might be located
Initial assessment once in the property	• Determine whether the person has a mental disorder, and how likely it is that the assessment will result in admission
	• Determine whether it is safe enough to complete the assessment in the person's home. If it isn't, provided that you are satisfied that the patient is likely to meet the requirements, ask the police to remove the person to a place of safety
	• If it is safe enough for the assessment to take place in the property, the issue is then whether the person (and anyone else mentioned in table 2.4 above) is willing to agree to the assessment taking place in their home
	• If the person lacks the ability to give agreement, permission cannot be obtained, and the person would need to be taken to another place of safety in order to complete the assessment

Timeline	Action
Completing assessment	• Once it has been established that an assessment is needed and where that assessment should take place, the assessment should be concluded as soon as practical • If the assessment takes place in the person's home, the 24 hours starts from the point where the police entered the property • A decision to move the person from their home after the beginning of the assessment should be based on the person's needs, not simply a matter of convenience. In the case of such a move, because this would be seen as a move between places of safety, the 24 hours will still begin from the point the police entered the property • A decision not to admit should include an alternative plan, and if necessary support to enable the person to remain in, or return home
Time limits for the use of warrants	Warrants must be used within three months from the date they were issued (but in practice should be used more promptly than that)

Transport to the place of safety

> Patients should always be transported in the manner which is most likely to preserve their dignity and privacy consistent with managing any risks
>
> CoP 17.3

This applies as much to taking someone to a place of safety as it does to taking them to hospital following an assessment.

Wherever possible, transport should be provided by an ambulance or other suitable vehicle rather than a police van. A police vehicle should only be used where information indicates other ways of transferring the patient would be too risky or impractical.

Arrival at the health-based place of safety under s136

Each area should have a local policy concerning who should receive and initially assess someone brought in on an s136. In some cases this may be an experienced psychiatric liaison nurse. However, even if seen by such a professional, a patient on s136 must also be seen by a doctor.

The AMHP on duty should be contacted as soon as possible (as police now have a duty – if practical – to consult mental health professionals prior to using their powers; this could also facilitate ensuring AMHPs are informed early).

If possible, the patient should be seen by an s12 doctor. It is also preferable for the AMHP and doctor to see the patient together to determine what treatment or care is needed.

If detention in hospital is a likely outcome, a second doctor must be involved. Who the second doctor is will depend on local protocol, but at least one of the two doctors must be section 12 approved.

In situations where the patient is seen first by a doctor, and they conclude that although the person is suffering from a mental disorder, they do not need admission, that person 'should still be seen by an AMHP' (CoP 16.51). This is to make sure that necessary arrangements for the patient's treatment or care are in place.

> ## Remember!
>
> If a doctor assesses the person and concludes that the person is not suffering from a mental disorder, then the person must be discharged even if not seen by an AMHP.
>
> CoP 16.50

s135(2)

This section will be used in circumstances where an person is already '**liable to be detained**' on section, but help is needed to take them (or return them) to hospital. For example:

- the person is on section, but is absent without leave (AWOL) from a ward;
- an assessment has been completed in the community but access to convey has been denied;
- where someone who is subject to a CTO has been recalled but is refusing to comply.

A warrant under s135(2) can be applied for by a police constable, or someone nominated by the hospital managers. In practice, local policy should determine who will apply for the warrant and who might appropriately accompany the police officers on execution of the warrant. It is unlikely to be an AMHP, unless they also happen to be the allocated key worker.

Identification and consultations with people holding key roles

Deciding who is the NR

The NR provides a significant protection to the patient, and has a number of powers. These include:

- the right to be informed about a decision to admit someone under s2;
- the right to be consulted about, and object to, the use of s3 and guardianship;
- the right to ask for the patient to be discharged (which can be blocked by the RC in charge of their treatment);
- the right to ask that an MHA assessment should be considered (and if it is decided that admission under section is not needed, to be told why)[3];
- the right to apply themselves for a patient's admission (where medical recommendations have been given, but the AMHP decides not to apply).

There are many ways to work out who the NR is. Here we describe one for those aged 18 plus, followed by one for under-18-year-olds. However, first of all, you need to consider whether the person is 'ordinarily resident' in the UK.

Remember!

People detained by the Courts under part three of the Act do not have a nearest relative.

The ordinary residence rule

This rule concerns the patient's country of residence. If a patient is '**ordinarily resident**' in the UK (i.e. this is their chosen home, for a settled period that has not come to an end) then you should follow all rules set out in each section.

If, however, the service user is visiting from abroad, or in your view still considers home to be abroad, you should ignore the rule that tells you to exclude any relative that doesn't live in this country (s26(5)(a)). This means that where both the patient and their NR usually live abroad, you don't need to exclude them when deciding who should be the NR.

Example from practice

Gerhunt (aged 19) came to London to study law. He has a diagnosis of bipolar disorder, and is seen by a psychiatrist in Germany when he returns home during term breaks.

Gerhunt is becoming acutely unwell. He has no partner and his mother (the older parent) is in Germany. You are happy that he is still ordinarily resident in Germany, within the meaning of the MHA, and you therefore treat Gerhunt's mother as his NR.

NR for people aged 18 plus

Make a list of anyone who falls within the following categories:

- husband, wife or civil partner;
- son or daughter;
- father or mother;
- brother or sister;
- grandparent;
- grandchild;
- uncle or aunt, or;
- nephew or niece.

Include:

- anyone who is living with the person (or lived with them prior to hospital admission) in an intimate relationship (girlfriend/boyfriend/partner) for six months or more, put first on the list, as they are seen as being 'married';
- anyone who they have shared a home with for five years or more, but not in an intimate relationship, add to the bottom of the list;
- anyone of 'half blood' (i.e. one common parent, one different);
- any legally adopted family members.

Now exclude:

- anyone aged under 18 years (unless they are married to the person);

- anyone who lives outside of the UK (unless the person themselves is ordinarily resident in another country, as explained above);
- anyone who would have been a wife/husband or civil partner, if they have permanently separated/divorced, etc.

Now prioritise:

- if there is a husband, wife, civil partner or equivalent still on the list, they will be the NR;
- if not, is there someone on the list who is living with or caring for the person? If yes, they are the nearest relative. If more than one person falls into this category, choose the person of full blood over half blood, then the eldest of the possible NRs;
- if not, choose the person highest on the list – they will be the NR. If there is more than one person in this category, (say a brother and a sister), choose someone of full blood over half blood, then the eldest.

Remember, gender is not a deciding factor, nor what the client might prefer.

Determining the nearest relative for someone aged under 18

The nearest relative of someone aged under 18 years is determined in the same way as anyone else, except:

- a parent must have parental responsibility (PR) in order to be considered (so mothers are always considered);
- only a married father (or an unmarried father named on the birth certificate) automatically has PR. Otherwise, an unmarried father must obtain a court order;
- if the young person is married (or living with someone as though they are married), their partner will be the NR, even if they are 16 or 17 years old;
- if the young person is in the care (with a care order, or interim care order) of the local authority, the local authority will be the NR (except if the young person is married);
- if someone has a special guardianship order, or a child arrangement order that specifies that the child should live with them, they will be the NR.

> Where there is more than one person who is a special guardian under the Children Act, all those with that status get to be the nearest relative. It is the only situation where more than one person can hold the NR role at the same time.
>
> s28 (1)

The conundrum of the five-year rule

This rule means that someone who wouldn't ordinarily be considered as a relative becomes one if they have been 'living with' the person for five years or more (for example, in a flat share). However, it is important to remember two things:

1 They would only move to the top of the list if there were no other relatives higher up the list who are 'living with' or 'caring for' the person.
2 The Reference Guide (2.11) clarifies that 'living with' means 'ordinarily residing with', in other words, the people who have freely chosen to live in the same home. This would therefore exclude people placed in residential care, or in prison, who cannot be said to have chosen where they are living.

Balancing rights and undertaking a 'good enough' consultation?

Particularly as far as the NR is concerned, you need to balance the client's rights to 'private and family life' (Article 8 rights[4]) with the obligation to consult to protect their 'right to liberty' (Article 5 rights) when considering s3 or s7, as well as the possible advantages of gaining useful information from others.

Consulting and notifying the nearest relative is a significant safeguard for patients.

Therefore decisions not to do so on these grounds should not be taken lightly. AMHPs should consider all the circumstances of the case, including:

- the benefit to the patient of the involvement of their nearest relative, including to protect the patient's Article 5 rights
- the patient's wishes including taking into account whether they have the capacity to decide whether they would want their nearest relative involved and any statement of their wishes they have made in advance. However, a patient's wishes will not be determinative of whether it is reasonably practicable to consult the nearest relative
- any detrimental effect that involving the nearest relative would have on the patient's health and wellbeing, and
- whether there is any good reason to think that the patient's objection may be intended to prevent information relevant to the assessment being discovered.

CoP 14.62

You therefore need to give the NR enough information about their relative's situation, so that they can play a meaningful part in the consultation process (*re Whitbread (Mental Patient: Habeas Corpus) [1998] and re Briscoe [1998]*).

When consulting nearest relatives AMHPs should, where possible:

- ascertain the nearest relative's views about both the patient's needs and the nearest relative's own needs in relation to the patient
- inform the nearest relative of the reasons for considering an application for detention and what the effects of such an application would be; and
- inform the nearest relative of their role and rights under the Act.

CoP 14.64

In an emergency situation it is possible to justify talking to an NR via a third party *(R v Managers of South Western Hospital)* – however, you need to be sure that that third party understands what the consultation entails – ideally therefore only an AMHP should be the third party. Having said that, whoever consults, the assessing AMHP retains responsibility for the consultation and should always consult personally if possible.

Remember!

If you have used a third party to consult, you can't sign the application form saying 'I have consulted' as this clearly wouldn't be true. In such a case, you should record the results of the 'consultation by proxy', and the reason for it, in your report. On the legal forms, you choose the section 'I have not' or 'I have not yet consulted the nearest relative'.

Informing and consulting

For admissions under s2, you must *inform* the NR of the admission. For admissions under s3 or s7 (guardianship), you must *consult* to ensure that the NR doesn't object to the use of compulsory powers. This does not mean that when considering the use of s2 you should not talk to the NR before conducting the assessment – this should be seen as good practice, rather than being a legal obligation.

Arguably, when consulting for s3 or s7 (guardianship) there are two stages:

1 The first stage is to provide sufficient information to allow the NR to make a meaningful contribution to the process.
2 The second stage is to ascertain whether the NR objects to the use of the compulsory power. It may be helpful to explain to NRs that not agreeing with you can be different from formally objecting.

> ## Example from practice
>
> When you talk to Mrs Jones about the possibility of her husband remaining in hospital subject to section 3 of the Act, she says she doesn't agree with your opinion about her husband needing to be in hospital. However, she thinks you, as the 'professional', should make the decision about whether or not to detain him under section 3. She makes it clear that she sees it as 'your' decision. Mrs Jones does not, therefore, formally object to the application.

When isn't it 'practicable' to consult the NR?

Once you have identified the NR, you *must* consult or inform if it is 'reasonably practicable' to do so. But what might 'not reasonably practicable' mean?

> Circumstances in which the nearest relative need not be informed or consulted include those where:
>
> - it is not practicable for the AMHP to obtain sufficient information to establish the identity or location of the nearest relative, or where to do so would require an extensive amount of investigation involving unreasonable delay, and
> - consultation is not possible because of the nearest relative's own health or mental incapacity.
>
> CoP 14.60

In other words, it may not be reasonably practicable under the following circumstances:

- You can't find out who the NR is – perhaps because the service user isn't willing to share this information.
- There is no one you can identify – perhaps because the service user is a refugee and has no relatives in this country.
- You know who the NR is, but can't get hold of them quickly enough – maybe they are on holiday or temporarily out of contact for some other reason.
- You do know who the NR is, but it isn't possible to communicate with them – for example, because they have advanced dementia.
- You know where and who the NR is, but, given the evidence available, you judge that the consultation would not be reasonably practicable because of the detrimental impact it would have on the client – perhaps because the NR abused them as a child. The acid test is whether a person's right to privacy under Article 8 of the Human Rights Act 1998 would be breached by consulting their NR, in a way that could not be defended on the grounds that it

was a proportionate response that was allowed for by law, and which protected their Article 5 rights to Liberty (because of the NR's ability to object to admission, and ask for discharge).

> ... Detrimental impact may include cases where patients are likely to suffer emotional distress, deterioration in their mental health, physical harm, or financial or other exploitation as a result of the consultation ...
>
> CoP 14.61

Because of this need to balance different aspects of someone's human rights, if you are contemplating not consulting, you should discuss this with your AMHP manager (whenever possible) and record your reasons carefully.

Even if you do decide that it isn't reasonably practicable to consult the NR, that person nevertheless remains the patient's NR. While you *may* talk to other relatives, they do not move 'up the list' and take over the NR position *unless:*

- it is delegated to them by the person who is the NR; or
- they are appointed as the NR by the Court.

If you decide not to inform or consult the NR because of the detrimental impact, it is important that you inform the MHA administrator at the receiving hospital of your decision. If you do not do so the MHA administrator may send statutory notifications to the NR, thereby informing the NR of the patient's admission and undoing your decision to protect the patient's privacy.

Example from practice

Ian has been assessed as needing admission to hospital. He has disclosed that his father sexually abused him. He has not disclosed to you who or where his father is.

Support is needed from the police to carry out the assessment. As part of the discussions on risk, information is shared with the police, and they reveal that they know Ian's father. He is being held in a local prison awaiting trial for a serious sexual assault on a minor.

You now know who and where Ian's father is – and presumably he is 'contactable'. However, given the history between father and son, after discussion with the AMHP duty manager, you agree it is not reasonably practicable to consult Ian's father, as to do so would cause Ian such significant distress that it would amount to a breach of his Article 8 right to privacy, and which could not be justified by the process set down by the law, which would protect his Article 5 rights to liberty.

Talking and listening to other people

People often have a range of individuals in their lives who can help us understand them, and the impact that a mental disorder is having on them. This could include:

- friends;
- other relatives;
- parents (where a child is on an interim care order, so would not be consulted as the nearest relative);
- advocates;
- carers and other professionals.

In deciding whether it is appropriate to consult carers and other family members, AMHPs should consider:

- the patient's wishes
- the nature of the relationship between the patient and the person in question, including how long the relationship has existed, and
- whether the patient has referred to any hostility between them and the person in question, or there is other evidence of hostility, abuse or exploitation.

CoP 14.68

Other views that need to be taken into account

With the advent of the MCA, there are others whose views you should also seek, in particular:

- people with an LPA that relates to psychiatric treatment;
- a Deputy from the Court of Protection;
- the person's representative, where someone is held by virtue of a standard or urgent DoL order.

Although the MHA doesn't provide a duty to consult these people, unless you do consider their views where they exist you will not be in a position to make an informed judgement based on all the available information.

Example from practice

Ellie has given her friend Josh a valid Lasting Power of Attorney relating to health and welfare. Josh knows that Ellie would not want to be given ECT[5]

> treatment in any circumstances and has made it known that he would
> exercise his right to refuse on her behalf.
>
> If at the point of assessment Ellie is happy to receive other treatment
> (and you don't believe she is being detained) you may decide that the
> use of the MHA is not necessary or appropriate, as she is not object-
> ing to other forms of treatment and ECT could not be given in
> these circumstances, even under MHA detention (except in
> an emergency).

So who should you consult and when? Table 2.6 compares the powers of the
different roles and what consultations have to take place.

Table 2.6 Who should be consulted and when?

	Nearest relative	Deputy or donee of LPA*
Must be consulted about informal admission	No	No
Would be good practice to be consulted about informal admission	Yes	Yes
Can object to informal admission	No	Yes (if the patient lacks capacity)
Can object to particular treatments for mental disorder while patient is informal	No	Yes (if the patient lacks capacity)
Must be consulted about admission under s2	No	No
Would be good practice to be consulted about compulsory admission under s2	Yes	Yes
Must be informed about admission under s2	Yes	No
Would be good practice to inform about admission under s2	N/A	Yes
Can object to admission under s2	No	No
Must be consulted about admission under s3	Yes	No
Would be good practice to be consulted about admission under s3	N/A	Yes
Can object to admission under s3	Yes	No

Note: *This assumes that the patient, when they had capacity, included the requirement that
the person who would take on the LPA should be kept informed of their treatment.

> ### Remember!
>
> You must consult the following people when considering admission for:
>
> - A ward of Court – an application in respect of a ward of court cannot be made without leave of the High Court (section 33(1)).
> - An MP – you must have permission of The Speaker of the House of Commons to proceed.
> - Someone with diplomatic immunity – this can include family and household members as well as the diplomat themselves. The Mental Health Act does not apply to those with diplomatic immunity. Contact the Foreign and Commonwealth office (Diplomatic Missions and International Organisations Unit) on 020 7008 1012 if you come into contact with someone who may have such immunity. The office can confirm their status and advise on how to proceed.

Advance decisions

An advance decision provides **competent adults** with a way of influencing the medical treatment that they might receive if they lose the capacity to make treatment decisions in the future. (See MCA Code of Practice for more information.) To be valid, the advance decision must:

- have been made when the person was aged *18 or over, and had the mental capacity* to make the given decision.

To be applicable, the advance decision must:

- be used at a point where the person *lacks capacity* to make the decision needed about medical treatment;
- be *applicable* to the treatment or situation the person wants to avoid, i.e. they need to be *explicit* enough about the treatment that it refers to (e.g. by saying that they don't want to be given a particular drug);
- not contradict an *expressed but different* opinion at a later point in time (which would invalidate the previously stated advance decision).

(See Chapter 1 'The legal landscape' for more information.)

> ### Example from practice
>
> Bruce's mother (and nearest relative) tells you that the previous Christmas he had stated adamantly that he never wanted to be given Prozac again – the side effects when he started were so awful.

However, the community psychiatric nurse reported that, as Bruce's mood improved after the New Year and into the spring, he told her that taking the anti-depressant had been 'worth the pain'. Given this information, the AMHP felt the earlier advance decision to refuse treatment with Prozac could not be relied upon because Bruce had changed his mind later on.

The effect of LPAs and advance decisions

Because LPAs and advance decisions provide an 'alternative decision-making process' at the point where a service user lacks capacity to make their own decisions, it is important for AMHPs and doctors to know about whether such 'decision makers' exist when considering whether it is 'necessary' to detain someone under the MHA.

Physical health care decisions and detained service users

It is important to remember that advance decisions and people holding appropriate LPA powers can influence a range of treatment decisions – including decisions about treatment for physical health problems not associated with any mental disorder. Such decisions will still have effect even if the patient is detained in hospital under the MHA.

Example from practice

Janice (40) has had schizophrenia since her teens. Two years ago Janice developed breast cancer. Despite aggressive intervention, the cancer has now spread to her bone marrow. While she still had capacity, she made an advance decision in writing and witnessed by her oncologist stating that she did not want to have any further treatment except palliative care, even if treatment could prolong her life. Subsequently Janice has become very psychotic and her GP has asked for an MHA assessment. As part of the process of the assessment, the AMHP consults the oncologist and realises that the advance decision exists. This is then taken into account in the decision-making process, as although Janice could be admitted under the MHA and her psychotic symptoms treated, she could not be given any treatment related to her breast cancer, unless circumstances exist that she had not previously taken account of (in which case the advance decision could have failed the applicability test).

Finding out whether either power exists is therefore an essential part of the preparations for an MHA assessment. However, the emphasis is on making 'reasonable efforts' to find appropriate information. An advance decision written and stored within a sock drawer in the back of a spare bedroom, for example, could not be found with 'reasonable effort', and an AMHP or other professional could not be blamed for not knowing about it.

Delegation and displacement of the nearest relative functions (2.25 Reference Guide)
Delegation and **displacement** are the two methods by which it is possible to change the person who needs to be consulted about MHA assessments and other relevant decisions. Delegation is covered by s32(2) and regulation 24.

Remember!

Delegation allows the nearest relative to nominate someone else to take on the role, but the identity of the nearest relative stays the same, and they can change their mind and take back the responsibilities of the nearest relative at any time. Displacement, on the other hand, allows a court to change the identity of the nearest relative, and in some cases you might need to go back to court if you wanted to change the nearest relative to someone else.

Delegation checklist

Things to remember when you are thinking about suggesting that the NR delegates their authority to make decisions under the MHA:

✓ The delegation must be in writing (but can be communicated electronically, for example using email or fax).

✓ The nearest relative can choose anyone (including someone not related to the service user) *except* the patient themselves *and/or* someone excluded under s26(5), i.e. (i) a divorced or separated partner; or (ii) someone who doesn't live in this country (where the patient does live here permanently); or (iii) someone under the age of 18 years; *or* someone who has previously been displaced by the courts. The exception to this second rule is where a court order has been obtained because there is no nearest relative (or none could reasonably be found).

✓ The letter or form must be sent to the person to whom the nearest relative wishes to delegate the powers, and will come into effect when that person receives it. (However, as the consent of the 'nominee' to taking on the role is needed, confirmation of acceptance from the nominee is helpful.)

✓ The relative must also let the patient know about this change.

✓ Make sure you change database information, and keep copies of delegation agreements on file.

See Table 2.7 for who needs to be informed about the delegation.

Table 2.7 Authorities to be notified by nearest relatives when they delegate functions or revoke delegation

Patient who is	Authority to be informed of the delegation or its revocation
detained in hospital	the managers of the hospital in which the patient is **liable to be detained**
a CTO patient	the managers of the responsible hospital
subject to guardianship	the responsible LSSA and (if applicable) the private guardian

Source: Reference Guide to the MHA table 6

Remember!

How or when delegation would end:

Either the original NR takes back their powers.

Or the original (delegating) NR changes, for example because the patient marries or the NR dies.

Or the Court agrees to displace the *delegating* NR in favour of someone else.

Remember!

Delegation could be seen as a positive alternative to displacement. For example, where a service user is considering asking that their NR be displaced, encouraging them to first approach the NR to consider delegation may prove less stressful and certainly less expensive than going to court.

Displacement s29

Who can displace the nearest relative?

- the patient
- any relative of the patient
- anyone who lives with the patient
- an AMHP.

Table 2.8 The grounds for displacement

The grounds	What it means
The patient doesn't have an NR	You have tried to find an NR but none exists. You may consider asking the County Court to appoint someone, particularly in situations where the service user lacks capacity and has no one else to speak up on their behalf
The NR can't take on the role because they are themselves ill	This includes physical as well as mental illness. For example, a patient whose NR father has dementia, may decide to displace him and suggest someone else. Then, when he is admitted, someone he trusts is there to protect his interests
The NR unreasonably objects to a service user's compulsory admission or the use of guardianship	This is the most common grounds used. However, it is important to remember you will need to show evidence to the judge about why you think the NR is being unreasonable
The NR has discharged the service user from hospital or guardianship without considering the consequences for the patient or the public	Sometimes used in addition to the grounds above, this section is really concerned about risk to the service user or others
The NR is 'otherwise unsuitable' for the role	For example, because the patient was abused by the NR, or would be distressed by their involvement; or because their relationship is distant or irrevocably broken down (see CoP 5.14)

Example from practice

Mary is unhappy with her father being her NR. She was abused by him (and he was imprisoned for this.) She considered delegation, but does not trust her father to choose someone. Mary therefore approaches the County Court, asking that they displace her father in favour of her brother Claude, on the basis that her father is 'unsuitable' as his involvement distresses her. If successful, the displacement will result in her father ceasing to be the NR and her brother becoming her NR instead.

Things to consider when displacement is suggested:

- Make sure you have identified the correct NR!
- Make time to talk to the NR, or support the patient to do so if this is appropriate. If they are objecting to admission, what is their reason? Is it really unreasonable? How would you convince the court of your point of view? What evidence do you have? It may be possible to find a compromise;

relatives may be reassured by talking things through with you, and reassess their objections, or be willing to consider not agreeing with you, but also not formally objecting.

- If it's the patient requesting the change, would delegation be a possibility for all parties?

Remember!

In all cases, the decision to make an application lies with the AMHP personally. CoP 5.15

This means the AMHP must reach their own decision. They cannot be 'told' to displace someone.

Process for displacement
When to consider it:

- The patient is on s2, and the NR is unreasonably objecting to s3 (remember an application in these circumstances extends the s2 until the court makes a final decision).
- The patient is in the community, you don't think a s2 could reasonably be used, and the NR is objecting to admission using s3.
- You want to consider guardianship and the NR either objects or is likely to discharge the person from the order unwisely.
- The CoP (5.12) also advises displacement should be considered where there is no NR, or the NR is unable to act due to illness/disability; and where there is good reason to think the patient would like to displace an unsuitable NR, but for some reason can't do so themselves.

Checklist: displacement

✓ The legal team responsible for helping AMHPs to undertake the displacement procedures is the LSSA legal team which authorises them. So the LSSA's legal department will help you make the application and check your reports. They will ask for an affidavit from you (a legal statement of facts) giving the reasons why displacement is necessary.

✓ Consider who should be the NR. The court will expect you to recommend a suitable person in your application (although you don't have to do so) so think about who it should be in advance. You can nominate more than one person.

✓ The court needs to be satisfied the person is 'suitable and willing', so if recommending someone, make sure you provide evidence of this.

✓ In the absence of any other friends or relatives able and appropriate to take on the task, you might want to consider using an advocate such as an Independent Mental Health Advocate (IMHA) to fill the role so that the service user's rights are protected. It is still possible for the LSSA itself to take on the role of NR, but in most cases, it is likely that someone else could do it. If the LSSA itself is nominated as the NR, a senior member of staff, independent of the team within which the applying AMHP is based, could be nominated to take on the role, so that functions such as consultations can be appropriately fulfilled. It is important that whoever takes on the role understands the powers and responsibilities.

If the County Court (or another court on appeal) decides to make an order, the order must specify who is to be the acting nearest relative. That must be:

- either the person (or one of the people) nominated in the application, if the court considers them to be a suitable (and willing) person to act as the patient's nearest relative; or
- if there is no such person, any other person whom the court considers is suitable (and willing) to do so.

2.48 Reference Guide to the Mental Health Act

Process at the court

The following is the process for lodging the application:

- The LSSA's lawyers will do this on your behalf (but not usually if the service user is the applicant).
- It is important to remember that *you* are the applicant, not the LSSA. The application should have your name on it.
- The application is made to the County Court.
- Except in an emergency, the court must provide the existing NR with copies of the papers and at least two days' notice so that they can organise a defence if they want to.
- In an emergency you provide what is called an 'ex-parte' application – in other words without the NR having to be provided with information in advance.
- If the patient is currently on s2, applying for displacement will 'freeze' the s2 until the case has been decided.
- It is important to reach a speedy conclusion about a displacement when an s2 is frozen as the patient cannot apply to a Mental Health Review Tribunal (MHRT) in the usual way. They would have to apply to the Secretary of State. If they lack capacity to decide whether to do so themselves, the hospital managers or local authority may do so on their behalf.

Table 2.9 Length of orders

Discharge on the basis of	Length of time
There isn't an NR The NR is too unwell to hold the role The NR is 'otherwise unsuitable'	**Either** it lasts for the period stated in the original order **Or** it can continue indefinitely, unless the patient, the new NR or the original NR go back to court and ask for a change Even if the appointed NR dies, the case would need to go back to court (see ref guide 2.57–59)
The NR had unreasonably objected to the application The NR had discharged the patient without considering their or others' welfare	**Either** it will last for three months from the time the order was made **Or** if the patient was detained in hospital or on a CTO at the time of the s29 Order, the order will end when the section ends

- The s2 extends until the application is disposed of by the court – that is, until:
  - the application for displacement is withdrawn; or
  - NR has chosen not to appeal, and the period for appeal has expired; or
  - the appeal has been decided or withdrawn.

Giving evidence in court

The local authority should ensure someone is there to support you. You may be expected to talk about your evidence, and the current NR or their solicitor will have a chance to cross-examine you if they wish.

How long do the orders last?

This depends on the reason why the displacement was agreed (see Table 2.9).

Checklist

The powers/rights the delegated/acting NR has are:

✓ to be consulted or informed about admission, and to object to the use of s3 or s7

✓ to apply themselves for admission under s2, 3, 4 or 7

✓ to be sent information about the admission or proposed discharge (subject to the patient not objecting)

✓ to request discharge from orders – including from s2, 3, 7 and 17A (with s7 – guardianship, the power to discharge is absolute – i.e. the local authority cannot block the request and their only option would be to consider displacement, if appropriate)

Where powers are limited:

✓ Where orders are imposed by the courts, the nearest relative's right to apply to a tribunal cannot be delegated, and neither can the right to be sent information.
✓ People held on forensic orders (s35 or s36) do not have a nearest telative (Reference Guide 14.24).

Meet the team

Every MHA assessment requires a team of people to undertake it. The make-up of the team can depend on the circumstances of the person you are assessing, but here are some general rules:

• Assessments for s2 or s3 and guardianship (s7): AMHP plus two doctors, one of whom must be a specialist psychiatrist approved under s12 of the Mental Health Act.
• Assessments for s4: AMHP plus one registered doctor (the doctor need not be s12 approved).
• Assessment for CTO (s17A): RC – who may or may not be a doctor – plus an AMHP.

Choosing the most appropriate assessors

There are three aspects that need to be considered here:

1 the relevance of experience of the team members to the person being assessed;
2 whether there are any conflicts of interest;
3 making sure the doctors who complete the assessment meet the s12 requirements.

Considering the relevance experience of team members

Where a patient is known to belong to a group for which particular expertise is desirable (e.g. they are aged under 18 or have a learning disability), at least one of the professionals involved in their assessment should have expertise in working with people from that group, wherever possible.

CoP. 14.39

Clearly, in some circumstances your choices will be limited. For example, with an assessment for CTO the other assessor has to be the responsible clinician for the service user being considered. Wherever you have the opportunity, select assessors who are most appropriate to the needs of the service user.

Considering potential conflict of interests and independence when choosing the assessing team

> AMHPs may not make an application if they have a potential conflict of interest as defined in the Mental Health (Conflicts of Interest) (England) Regulations 200856 and described in figure 37. An application made by an AMHP who had a potential conflict of interest would be invalid and would not provide any authority for the patient's detention.
>
> Reference Guide 8.55

S12A of the MHA includes regulations about what would amount to a conflict of interest. Conflicts fall into four categories:

- financial
- business
- professional
- personal.

The rules concerning conflicts of interest apply to all members of the assessing team, that is, both the AMHP and the doctors. This includes assessments for s2, s3, s4 or s7 (guardianship). They *do not* apply to assessments for CTOs.

Although there are specific issues which would exclude an assessor, it is also important to consider these areas more generally, and where you think that there may be an 'appearance' of a conflict, even if it is not explicitly forbidden, assessors should consider whether to withdraw from the assessment.

> Assessors should work on the principle that in any situation where they believe that the objectivity or independence of their decision is (or could be seen to be) undermined then they should not become involved or should withdraw.
>
> CoP 39.15

Financial conflicts

Financial conflicts arise where an assessor may make a financial gain or loss as a result of the assessment. The exception is the payment of a fee for the assessment. In addition, so long as other areas of conflict do not arise, it is acceptable for one (but not more than one) doctor to be on the staff of a private hospital in circumstances where the assessors are considering whether to admit to that hospital.

The Code 39.4 (clarified by the Reference Guide p.6) suggests that it would be good practice to avoid using two doctors who are based on the same hospital trust site. However, it is important to remember that there will be times when you will need to depart from this 'good practice' guidance in the Code. You can do so as long as you do not 'fall foul' of what the regulations say.

Example from practice

Rita had arranged to assess Abbas with the team consultant psychiatrist, and an independent s12 doctor. At the last minute, the s12 doctor pulled out. Due to the risks in the case, rather than delay further, Rita asked another consultant psychiatrist who worked at the same hospital to attend. She checked there were no other line management or other conflicts and was satisfied there were not. In her AMHP report, she explained what had happened, and that although she could not follow the 'good practice' guidance of the Code, she was satisfied she had abided by the regulations and the detention was therefore legal.

Business conflicts

Business conflicts relate to circumstances where two or more assessors are closely involved in a business venture. For example, two GP partners in a practice could not both make recommendations for the same MHA assessment. However, such business interests need not have anything to do with health or social care. For example, if two doctors started a business between them (say 'rock climbing for beginners') even though this had nothing to do with mental health it would be sufficient to count as a conflict of interest.

Professional conflicts

Such conflicts are concerned with the potential impact of professional relationships on decision-making. The regulations mention three specific circumstances where a conflict will exist:

- One assessor is in a line management or employment relationship with another assessor.
- The patient and one or more assessor work in the same team.
- All three assessors work together in the same team. A 'team' in this context refers to 'a group of professionals who work together for clinical purposes on a routine basis'.

There is one exception to this final rule concerning three assessors – this means that in a case of 'urgent necessity', the three assessors *can* work in the same team. However, the other areas of conflict must still be satisfied. So for example, in a circumstance where there were two doctors and an AMHP in a team, with one doctor the line manager/clinical supervisor of the other, even in a case of urgent necessity the three professionals could not assess together because there would still be a professional conflict (a line management relationship) between the two doctors.

Personal conflicts

Personal conflicts relate to personal relationships between assessors – by marriage, blood or other in law or kinship relationships either currently or in the past. Assessors do not have to be married for there to be a potential conflict, and divorce would not mean a personal conflict no longer existed. So if an assessor were asked to assess the sister of an ex-husband or wife, this would be as much a conflict as would be the case were they still married.

Conflicts of interest and community treatment orders

The regulations do not apply to assessments for a CTO (or its revocation). However the advice of the Code is that neither the AMHP nor RC should have a financial interest in the outcome of the assessment. Additionally, there should be no personal relationships between the AMHP, RC or the patient.

Conflicts of interest and renewal of detention and guardianship

Although the regulations do not formally apply to these renewals, as with CTOs those professionals responsible for these decisions should be conscious of any potential conflicts, particularly those related to finances.

The important thing to remember is that all assessors are expected to reach independent decisions, and if any one assessor felt that they were being placed under pressure to make a decision in a particular way they should consider withdrawing and should in any case raise the issue. For example, an AMHP should raise the issue with their professional lead or approving authority.

Making sure the doctors meet the s12 requirements

S12 sets out the legal requirements of s12 – basically what experience or qualifications doctors completing a MHA must have. The summary below is taken from 8.40 of the Reference Guide (figure 36: medical recommendations)

> **What 'previous acquaintance' means:**
>
> At least one of the doctors should, if practicable, have had previous acquaintance with the patient. Preferably, this doctor should have treated the patient personally, but case law has established that previous acquaintance need not involve personal acquaintance, provided the doctor in question has some knowledge of the patient and is not 'coming to them cold'.
>
> 8.40 CoP

Table 2.10

One doctor	Other doctor
	If the doctor approved under section 12 does not have previous acquaintance with the patient:
Approved under section 12	If practicable, a doctor who has previous acquaintance with the patience.
	Otherwise:
	Any doctor

Checklist: Assessors

✓ You will need the recommendations from two doctors prior to completing applications for s2, 3 or 7 (one doctor for s4).

✓ To make a community treatment order you need the agreement of the responsible clinician for the patient plus an AMHP.

✓ For a CTO, if the in-patient RC and Community RC are different people, it would be good practice to involve both in the decision-making.

✓ At least one of the two doctors involved in initial detentions must be s12 approved.

✓ Where practicable, at least one of the two medical recommendations should be given by a doctor who knows the service user. The GP is the obvious choice.

✓ Doctors who do not know the patient should, if possible, be s12 approved.

✓ 'Knowing' meanings having at least some previous knowledge of the patient, preferably from having treated the patient themselves, but potentially from notes (CoP 14.73).

✓ The rules around conflicts of interest apply to the AMHP as well as the doctor.

✓ The conflict of interest rules apply to all assessments *except* assessments for CTOs (but the Code still advises that conflicts around finances and personal relationships to the patient should be avoided).

✓ Where the patient is to be admitted to, or continues to remain in, an independent hospital, it is possible for one of the recommendations to be made by a doctor on the staff of the hospital (as long as they do not 'fall foul' of other areas of conflict, such as personal conflicts).

✓ Where the two doctors are employed by the same Trust, it is good practice for them to be based at different sites (but remember, as this is advice from the Code, and not contained within the regulations, this advice can be departed from where you have good reason).

✓ It is not possible to make a recommendation or application where the person being assessed works within the same team as, or is employed by, one of the assessors.

✓ The emphasis is on the assessor making a reasoned, ethical decision about whether or not there might be a conflict of interest, or the perception of a conflict of interest. The advice of the Code (39.15) is that if you feel that there may be a conflict of interest, you should not take part in the assessment.

The Act requires an AMHP to take an independent decision about whether or not to make an application under the Act. If an AMHP believes that they are being placed under undue pressure to make, or not make, an application, they should raise this through the appropriate channels. Local arrangements should be in place to deal with such circumstances.

CoP 39.18

✓ It is the job of the AMHP, and indeed other professionals, to make reasoned decisions in a spirit of cooperation and independence. If you feel you are being pressurised into making an inappropriate decision, raise the issue with the AMHP lead for your organisation.

Remember!

If you make an application, or a recommendation, where there is a clear conflict of interest, as defined by the regulations, *the detention will not be valid.*

The role and tasks of independent mental health act advocates in MHA assessments[6]

The 1983 Mental Health Act as amended in 2007 created the role of independent mental health advocate (IMHA). IMHAs have a clear statutory role alongside other professionals involved in the process of assessing and treating patients. Advocacy is well established within mental health services, and the role of an IMHA complements that of generic advocacy services and fits within the same set of principles.

The key aspects of the role are:

- independence
- empowerment
- impartiality
- confidentiality

- inclusion
- free access.

IMHAs are specialist advocates who are trained to support qualifying patients who are subject to the powers of the MHA. Those eligible to the services of an IMHA are:

- those detained under the Act (with some exceptions in an emergency);
- those on Supervised Community Treatment;
- those subject to guardianship;
- conditionally discharged restricted patients;
- some informal patients under s57 and under 18s being considered for treatment to which s58A applies.

The Code of Practice outlines the role of IMHAs and this is a good starting point for AMHPs when they are working alongside an IMHA. IMHAs have a duty to help patients understand:

- their rights under the Act;
- the parts of the Act that apply to them;
- the rights other people have in relation to the Act (e.g. NR);
- any medical treatment they are receiving or may receive.

As an IMHA only has statutory powers in relation to the above issues, a generic advocate or another agency may still be or need to be involved. If an IMHA does support a patient on wider issues then they do not have legal powers (for example, the powers they have in relation to seeing patient records).

Remember!

The following people can ask for an IMHA to visit a patient:

- an AMHP
- the patient's RC
- the NR.

However, it is the service user's decision whether or not they wish to use the service.

How an IMHA might help professionals during MHA assessments

IMHAs should help patients understand their rights under the Act, in particular those that apply to them, and the rights of others involved in the assessment process (i.e. the NR's right to ask for an assessment, and to request their discharge).

If requested by the patient, IMHAs can also obtain information that enables the patient to understand the process and any medical treatment they are receiving or may receive. In stressful and confrontational situations like an MHA assessment, IMHAs may not only help the patient to express their views, they may also be in a better position to give an explanation of what is happening, or will happen next, to the patient. This may be more acceptable to the patient rather than coming directly from the AMHP as, despite the independence of the AMHP role, patients can see them as a negative part of the assessment process. IMHAs and other advocates are most likely to be involved in pre-planned assessments, for example when a patient is on an s2 and an assessment for s3 is being planned, or where a patient on s3 is being considered for a CTO. When planning such an assessment an AMHP should consider asking if a detained patient has access to or would like an IMHA to be with them during the assessment to offer support.

Working with IMHAs in assessments

Remember!

IMHAs have the right to visit and talk to a patient in private. AMHPs can support this by ensuring an appropriate space is available.

In contrast to the power held by AMHPs, IMHAs have no power in the assessment process and can only stand alongside to enable the patient to be heard. This can make a big difference to the patient involved. In the process of any assessment there will be an inevitable tension between maintaining the independence of the IMHA role and the independence of the AMHP role. While both are independent an IMHA can only represent the views and wishes of the patient, however rational or otherwise. It is not the AMHP's, or any other professional's, role to try to persuade an IMHA otherwise but only to provide information to enable the IMHA to best represent the wishes of their client.

Remember!

IMHAs provide a safeguard for patients who are receiving or being assessed for compulsory treatment.

The onus is on professionals to inform (qualifying) patients of the existence of IMHAs and how to access them. Although it is the managers of the hospital (or the LSSA for guardianship) who have the legal duty to inform patients of their rights to access the service, clearly it would be good practice for AMHPs to do so too. Additionally, AMHPs have a right to refer a service user to the IMHA service. So in a situation where the patient lacks capacity to ask for themselves, but the AMHP feels that they would benefit from the service, a referral should be considered.

✓
Checklist: involvement of IMHAs in MHA assessments

Before assessing a patient, consider:

✓ Do you have the contact details for your local advocacy project?
✓ Has the patient asked for an advocate?
✓ Have you explained the role and benefits of using an IMHA service?
✓ Is there somewhere the IMHA can talk to the patient in private?
✓ Does the IMHA need any information to represent their client?

Thinking ahead: resources

A key part of the AMHP role concerns mobilising appropriate resources, both as an alternative to admission, and to make sure that the resources you need at or soon after the assessment are in place. Possible resources include the following:

✓
Checklist: resources that may be needed during an MHA assessment

✓ Locksmith to enter if appropriate and strategy to secure property if needed, or access to a key plus warrant if possible
✓ Arrangements to look after children or adults with care and support needs if needed
✓ Arrangements to look after pets if needed
✓ Access to friends or other professionals if patient has requested their presence in the past during MHA assessments
✓ Having the right doctors!
✓ Ambulance control contact number
✓ Police (present, if you need them, or aware that you are out there without them)
✓ Getting the right bed sorted
✓ Interpreters for people who are deaf or for whom English is not their first language
✓ Involvement of the Crisis Resolution/Home Treatment Team as appropriate

Sourcing the most appropriate bed to meet the needs of the patient
Although it is Health's responsibility to locate a suitable bed, it is wise to think ahead for two reasons:

1 It will save you time later in the assessment.

2   You won't be able to make an application until you know where the bed is based as you must state the hospital to which the patient will be admitted, not just the Trust, on the application form – and if you are considering using an s3, the doctors cannot make their recommendations unless they can confirm that appropriate treatment is available and *where* it is to be provided.

Checklist: finding the right bed

The following groups of service users need special consideration when thinking about beds:

✓ **People over 65 years.** There may be a separate service, with a separate bed manager. There can be an issue when the service user has a mental illness such as schizophrenia, or is particularly agitated, because most services for people over 65 years are targeted towards vulnerable and frail service users with dementia. Such services find it harder to cope with 'younger' patients (i.e. active 65–75-year-olds), and will need more background and risk information to ensure that they have appropriate extra support in place. The emphasis should be on finding the right place for the patient.

✓ **Mothers and babies.** Mothers with babies under 1 year should be kept together whenever possible. Trusts tend to have contracts with a regional mother and baby unit, but these can be full. When working with a client who is pregnant and also has mental health needs, it is worth encouraging doctors (if need be) to involve other services early.

✓ **People with eating disorders.** Again, a specialist service is not provided directly by every Trust. Also, different units can have different attitudes towards using the MHA to compel someone with an eating disorder to have treatment.

✓ **People with learning difficulties.** Trusts often maintain a few beds with trained staff for people with a learning disability and in need of treatment for a mental disorder. Since the Winterbourne Scandal, there have also been attempts to place people closer to home. Beds for people with challenging behaviour are more difficult to locate. Encouraging services to consider this need early is essential. Locating and talking to the appropriate commissioner can be very helpful.

✓ **People with personality disorders.** New services have been developed in the last few years to cater for the special needs of this group. A number of services won't accept patients who are compulsorily detained. Often people 'end up' on general adult wards. It is worth checking local agreements.

✓ **Young people under the age of 18 years.** The law aims to stop young people under the age of 18 years being admitted onto unsuitable adult wards for assessment or treatment of mental disorder. However, it is not illegal for an under-18-year-old to be on an adult ward, but they will need appropriate support and safeguards if this is the only safe option. 'Tier 4' (i.e. inpatient beds for those under 18 years) can be in particularly short supply, and are rarely agreed for emergency admissions. Local children's wards in acute hospitals are often used to fill the gap. Make sure you know what the arrangements are locally for assessments and admissions of young people.

Remember!

Under-18-year-olds should be admitted to accommodation that is 'suitable for their age (subject to their needs)'. These rules apply whether or not the child or young person is formally detained. What this means is that the primary consideration should be the young person's age, but there will occasionally be situations where the needs of the child or young person can only be met on a ward designed for adults. In such cases additional specialist staff should be available on the ward to support the young person.

(See CoP chapter 19 for more details.)

Use the table in Appendix 1 to write down the local contacts for these specialist groups of patients.

Checklist: last minute checks for MHA assessments

✓ Location and phone number of the patient, and their nearest relative or family/friends
✓ Arrangements for meeting any other professionals involved in the assessment
✓ Involvement of the police and knowledge of any relevant risk information
✓ Ambulance has been booked if possible or number available to call them if not
✓ You have copies of legal papers (including s4, and NR's application forms)
✓ If you might need to submit an application remotely (by email) you have the correct email address
✓ You have a s135 warrant if appropriate
✓ Doctors are contactable if necessary
✓ Location of ward or resource as appropriate
✓ Telephone number of bed manager in case of problems
✓ Telephone number of ward in case of problems
✓ Telephone number of senior/duty manager in case of problems!
✓ And finally – take some nourishment with you and have a comfort break before you go out. Just in case!

Summary

- Effective preparation is key in any MHA assessment, whether you have five minutes or five days to prepare.
- Make sure you have as much information as possible, so that you are able to effectively assess the risks and make plans accordingly.
- Make sure you have talked to the NR, unless it is not practicable to do so, and any other relevant people who can help you form a full picture of the patient.
- As a minimum, you need to make sure you have assembled your assessing team, can get access to the patient, can safely complete the assessment with the support of the police (if needed), and will be able to assess the patient in an 'appropriate manner'.
- If possible make sure you know where the patient will be admitted to if needed, and take details of the bed manager, ward manager and AMHP lead or supervisor with you in case you run into any problems and need some help.

Notes

1   Information sharing: Advice for practitioners providing safeguarding services to children, young people, parents and carers. HM Government, July 2018.
2   Provided by Alison Greenhalgh and Shilpa Nariri Camden and Islington MHFT.
3   See Appendix 4 for full list of NR rights – taken from chapter 2 of the MHA Reference Guide.
4   The European Convention on Human Rights.
5   ECT is a treatment, mainly used for major depression in circumstances where either alternative treatments have not worked, or where there are physical health concerns as a result of the depression (e.g. not eating or drinking) and it would not be safe to wait for other treatments to have an effect.
6   This section is provided by Sarah Dewey, service user consultant.

3 Managing Mental Health Act assessments and making decisions

By the end of this chapter you should have an understanding of:

- How to manage the assessment, risk and people
- Making good explanations and introductions at the start of assessment
- Knowing how to work well with interpreters
- The legal criteria for admission under s2, s3 and s4
- The different factors that need to be taken into account when undertaking an assessment
- How to consider alternatives to admission
- Choosing between different sections of the MHA
- How to choose between the MHA and MCA (including DoLS) when making decisions

Managing the assessment, risk and people

Overview: coordinating the process

One of the main tasks of the AMHP in an MHA assessment is the management of the process of assessment. This includes making sure that the assessment happens in as safe a way as possible, and that it allows the people concerned, in particular patients and carers, to understand the process, and be as involved as they can and want to be.

> Unless different arrangements have been agreed locally by the relevant authorities, *AMHPs who assess patient for possible detention under the Act have overall responsibility for co-ordinating the process of assessment ...*
>
> CoP 14.41 (emphasis added)

Starting off

An important place to start is to ensure that everyone present in the assessment is aware of their roles, that you have decided who would be the most appropriate person to start speaking, and that you have decided how to effectively use the support of people outside of the assessing team. These people may include:

- a carer or other family member;
- friends, advocates or other supports;
- interpreters;
- the police or ambulance staff;
- other professionals who know the patient or family well (a care coordinator, for example).

With complex assessments involving a number of people, such as the police, it can be helpful to arrange to meet away from the assessment for a few minutes to plan your strategy, for example:

- Do you need the police with you in the property to maintain the peace and keep people safe, or would it be more helpful to have them waiting for you nearby? Who should enter first?
- Is the patient likely to feel more comfortable initially speaking to someone they know well, such as a GP or care coordinator? If you take this approach, how will you also ensure that the patient understands what is going on? Is it possible to ask the other person to make the introductions, but suggest they introduce you last so that you can explain about the process of assessment?
- If you can't talk to the nearest relative before the assessment, and know you will need to talk to them while the patient is nearby, how will you manage this? Would it work to say at the beginning of the assessment that you need to talk to them separately, or do you need to be more tactful, perhaps by asking the nearest relative to make the patient a drink, and going with them into the kitchen to 'help'?
- Does the patient have any special communication needs? For example, are they hard of hearing, or autistic? Is English their first language or do they (or any of the assessing team) have a strong accent which may get in the way of effective communication?

Remember!

It is important to be aware that different professionals will approach a situation from their own standpoint: police wish to keep the peace; doctors want to know if someone is really ill enough to need admission to hospital; AMHPs need to focus on ensuring they understand the patient's situation as part of

the 'whole picture' of their lives, empowering the person to have as construc-
tive a role as possible in the process. Ultimately the AMHP must reach a
decision about the need for the use of compulsory powers, such as CTO or
formal admission to hospital under the Act.

The authority to enter a place to search for someone who has a mental disorder s115

Approved mental health professionals (AMHPs), when acting as such on
behalf of a local authority, may at all reasonable times enter and inspect any
premises, including care homes and private dwellings, in which a mentally
disordered patient is living, if the AMHP has reasonable cause to believe that
the patient is not 'under proper care'.

Reference Guide 7.2

AMHPs have the authority under s115 of the Act to 'enter and inspect' places
when they are acting on behalf of the local authority. However, AMHPs can't
force entry or stay if asked to leave – and the power provided by s115 is vested
in the AMHP, not other members of the assessing team such as doctors or the
police. Once 'through the door' the first task of the AMHP is to make sure the
patient (and others, such as family members) understand what is happening,
and the possible outcomes of the assessment.

If you don't believe you will be able to gain access (or finish the assessment
safely in the property) you should consider applying for an s135 warrant. See
the previous chapter.

Introductions and explanations

At the start of an assessment, AMHPs should identify themselves to the
person being assessed, members of the person's family, carers or friends
and other professionals present. AMHPs should ensure that the purpose of
the visit, their role and that of the other professionals are explained. They
should carry documents with them at all times which identify them as AMHPs
and which specify both the LSSA which approved them and the LSSA on
whose behalf they are acting.

CoP 14.51

It is the AMHP's role to ensure that the service user is introduced to the assessors
and understands what is happening. This *must* happen in every assessment,
unless there is a good reason for it not to. If you feel for a particular reason
that an introduction needs to be curtailed or not given, you must explain why

in your report, bearing in mind the principles of the Code and the obligations under the HRA.

(2) – Everyone who is arrested shall be informed promptly, in a language which he understands, of the reasons for his arrest and any charge against him.

HRA: Article 5 – Right to Liberty and Security

Everyone has their own way of introducing an assessment but remember that your approach and language need to be tailored to fit the person's needs. Useful information to include could be:

- what is happening and why;
- who everyone in the assessment is, and their role;
- what needs to be decided, and by whom;
- how long the assessment may last, and whether you plan to take a break to discuss your decision with the other professionals.

Example from practice

Introducing an assessment to someone with an autistic spectrum disorder

Tony has a diagnosis of Asperger syndrome. This means he tends to think about situations in a very literal way, and finds language such as euphemisms confusing and anxiety-provoking. He also works better with visual images rather than the spoken word.

When making the introductions, the AMHP tells Tony that they are going to ask him some questions, because people who care about him, such as his parents, are worried because he appears to be more anxious than usual. The worker also tells Tony the order in which people will speak, and that after they have asked him questions, they will stop for a while and leave the room. She explains that this is so they can decide what to do next. She also explains that they have to decide if Tony needs any help, for example from nurses or social workers visiting him at home, or possibly coming into hospital.

As the worker describes these options, she draws them on a piece of paper for him. Stick people talking to him, then three options (hospital, home with support, no help with a question mark) so that he can see what they are suggesting, and finally, she draws three clock faces with the current time, the time they hope to finish the interview, then the time they will take to talk about what to do next.

This reassures Tony, who becomes less agitated.

What is a 'good enough' medical/ psychiatric assessment?

> A medical examination must involve:
>
> - direct personal examination of the patient and their mental state, and
> - consideration of all available relevant clinical information, including that in the possession of others, professional or non-professional.
>
> CoP 14.72

Clearly, the first thing to consider is whether you can have direct physical contact to complete the assessment. If you can't, consider delaying. Having said that, there may be situations where although you haven't directly spoken to the person, you still have enough direct observation of the evidence to allow you to make a decision.

Example from practice

Dr Liam (an independent s12 doctor) was asked to assess Craig in the police station, where he had been taken for breach of the peace. Dr Liam was able to talk to Craig's care coordinator and get information about his diagnosis of schizophrenia and the fact that he had been refusing to take his depot for three months. Once at the station, Liam met with the other doctor and AMHP and discussed Craig with the custody Sargent. She said that since being in the cell, Craig had been pacing constantly, muttering and appeared to be responding to something that wasn't there. When officers had attempted to enter the cell to talk to him, Craig had 'rushed' at them, screaming and trying to strike anyone within range. She showed them Craig on the monitors in the cells, and Dr Liam could see him pacing, muttering and gesticulating (for example, shaking his fist towards the far wall of the cell, and shouting obscenities). When the doctors and the AMHP attempted to enter the cell themselves, Craig rushed them, shouting and swearing. They had to slam the door to protect themselves. The Custody Sargent did offer to ask riot-trained officers to attend with shields so that they could safely open the door and contain Craig in a corner of the cell. However, Dr Liam (as well as the other assessors) felt this would be really scary and oppressive for Craig, and decided to conduct the interview through the open 'window' in the cell door. During this conversation, Craig, although clearly angry about being arrested, was also sharing delusional ideas about his parents (who were in fact in Australia) trying to poison him, and coming into the cell to laugh at him. Based on this interview, Dr Liam was satisfied that he had observed enough to make an informed decision about the fact that Craig did appear to be suffering from a mental disorder, and that further assessment was warranted in the interests of his own health and safety and the safety of others.

Checklist for doctors completing assessments (CoP 14.71–76)

✓ Direct physical contact is needed to make an assessment. If this isn't possible, consider asking the AMHP to get a warrant under s135. If it isn't safe to wait, consider involving the police and asking them to use their powers of entry under the Police and Criminal Evidence (PACE) Act. This may be possible where there is evidence of immediate risk to life.

In the Devon Partnership NHS Trust v SSHSC [2021] EWHC 101 (Admin) case, it was established that the words 'personally seen' by the AMHP in s11, and 'personally examined' by the doctors in s13 meant that there needed to be direct physical contact between assessors and the person being assessed for admission under s2, s3 or s4, or the use of guardianship under s7. In addition Derbyshire Healthcare NHS Foundation Trust vs SSHSC (2023) EWHC 3182 established that for renewals of s3, CTOs and Guardianship a remote assessment using a video link would not be sufficient.

✓ If 'practical', one doctor should know the patient, and one doctor must be s12 approved. If neither doctor knows the patient, it's better to have two s12 doctors.

✓ 'Knowing' the patient ideally means having treated them personally in the past, but can mean having at least had access to previous knowledge/notes about them.

✓ It isn't enough to just say a person has a particular diagnosis. You need to describe what you see – remember you need to evidence that the mental disorder is of a 'nature or degree' that warrants the use of the MHA, and the risks that are associated with the mental disorder as a result.

✓ For s3, you must be able to specify where appropriate treatment will be available. This can be as specific as a particular ward or unit, or as general as naming a number of hospitals that could provide such treatment. Remember: don't just name a trust.

Other practical things for doctors to remember

- It isn't the AMHPs responsibility to find a bed, it's a Health responsibility.
- You won't always agree with the AMHP, but if you don't, you still need to work together to think about alternative support plans (where needed).
- Be conscious of risks to the assessing team – and make sure no one person is left alone to manage them.

Interviewing in a 'suitable manner': when and how to use an interpreter

Clearly, if English is not a patient's first language, it is necessary to investigate whether or not an interpreter may be needed. An interpreter may also be needed when someone has a hearing impairment.

Remember!

When working with people who are deaf, wherever possible use a professional interpreter with recognised qualifications and supported references. British sign language interpreters should be registered with Council for Advancement of Communication with Deaf People (CACDP) and/or be members of the Association of Sign Language Interpreters.

Getting the right sort of interpreter is essential, including, for someone who has a hearing impairment, ensuring that the interpreter and the client use the same 'version' of sign language. For example, Deaf people from Eastern Europe use a different form of sign language, compared to their UK counterparts. It's good practice for AMHPs to be provided with appropriate training that helps develop their skills and knowledge and to promote best practice in working with interpreters. Even in situations where a person would usually be able to communicate clearly in English, an interpreter may be needed as some people tend to revert to their mother tongue when under stress. Therefore it is useful to check whether the person you need to interview is *currently* able to talk in, and understand English. If you start an assessment, and realise the person you are assessing is not able to communicate in the way you had expected, you should consider whether you can continue, or whether to reconvene when an interpreter is available.

Remember!

When working with interpreters less familiar with Mental Health Act assessments:

- Explain the process of assessment, so that the interpreter knows what to expect.
- Ask that they translates directly what is said – especially by the patient to you. The interpreter needs to not try to make what is said 'make sense'.
- It can be helpful to decide whether the interpreter should speak in the first or third person, i.e. as though it is them saying the words, or as though others are saying them.
- It is okay to stop the interview and review the process, if you are concerned that the interpreter may not be translating accurately. This can help things get 'back on track'.

It is useful to work with interpreters who are familiar with the mental health system and legislation – but this of course is not always possible. It is worth checking whether the interpreter has much experience in working in the mental health field.

Avoid 'telephone' interpreting services if at all possible. Interpreting in mental health act assessments is challenging in any situation – trying to do so where someone cannot see what is happening in the room is particularly difficult. If it is safe to do so, consider delaying the assessment until an appropriate interpreter is available.

Powers available under the civil sections of the MHA

Table 3.1 provides a quick reminder of the purpose and time limits for sections concerned with assessing and admitting people to hospital.

Table 3.2 provides equivalent information for sections used to support people in the community.

Table 3.1   Powers under the civil sections of the Mental Health Act 1983

Section	Related power	How long it lasts
s5(4)	Enables someone to be kept on a ward until it is possible for a doctor or approved clinician to assess them and decide whether assessment and detention under the MHA is necessary	Up to 6 hours
s5(2)	Enables doctors and approved clinicians to keep someone on a ward until an MHA assessment can be completed	Up to 72 hours
s136	Enables someone to be kept in a particular place, or taken to a particular place to enable a full MHA assessment to take place	Up to 24 hours plus a 12-hour extension
s135(1)	Enables AMHPs, supported by the police and at least one doctor, to enter someone's home (by force if necessary) to decide if a person needs to be assessed for admission under the MHA, and, if necessary, remove them to a place of safety to allow that assessment to take place	Up to 24 hours plus a 12-hour extension
s135(2)	Provides authority for the police to enter and return a patient to hospital who is already 'liable to be detained' (because an assessment has been completed, because they are AWOL from hospital, or because they have been recalled under CTO powers, but have refused to return to hospital) and return them to the place they are required to be	Because they are already 'liable to be detained', the time limits are those imposed by the section they are on

Table 3.1 *Continued*

Section	Related power	How long it lasts
s4	Enables an MHA assessment to happen outside of an inpatient ward in circumstances where only one doctor can be located, and it would be too risky to leave the patient while waiting for a second doctor to be available	Up to 72 hours
s2	Enables someone to be detained to allow ongoing assessment (or assessment followed by treatment) of a mental disorder	Up to 28 days
s3	Allows for the detention of a person for treatment for a mental disorder, where appropriate conditions are met	Up to six months (renewable for six months, then annually)

Remember!

In some areas, and at some times of the day, it can be difficult to locate a second s12 doctor. If you have a bed (so know you can admit the patient), it is worth considering whether the risks are such that it would be better to admit using s4, and arrange for the second doctor to see the patient after they have been admitted. Ideally, this first doctor should be one who knows the patient.

Example from practice

Sasha is an AMHP employed by an Emergency Duty Team in a rural county. He is called by a GP who had done a home visit to see a patient, Emma, who had given birth a few months ago. Emma had had a 'postpartum psychosis' after her first child, but had appeared to be doing okay this time around. Her husband had called the GP because he had become concerned that she wouldn't put the baby down at all, and kept insisting that she needed to leave the house to be safe, even though it was February, and a storm was expected. The GP and husband had been trying to persuade Emma to go to A&E, without success. Sasha couldn't locate an s12 doctor willing to come out (by this time it was 11pm), but the local hospital had a bed and were happy to admit. Sasha also contacted the local police, who agreed to offer support. As soon as Sasha arrived, it was evident that it wouldn't be possible to wait until morning – the risks were too high. The GP therefore made a recommendation under s4, and Sasha an application. With the help of police, Emma was admitted to hospital.

Table 3.2 Compulsion in the community

Section	Related power	How long it lasts
Mental Health Act 1983 s7	**Guardianship** Using compulsory powers to support a community care plan, providing requirements for person concerned to live in a certain place, to attend a place for occupation or treatment, and allow particular people to visit them at home	Up to six months (renewable for six months, then annually)
Mental Health Act 1983 s17A (community treatment order)	Community treatment orders (CTO): allows someone detained on s3 (or the equivalent **unrestricted forensic section**) to be discharged onto the order. The order allows the responsible clinician (with the agreement of an AMHP) to set conditions on the discharge, and recall the patient to hospital if appropriate	Six months (renewable for six months, then annually)
Mental Capacity Act 2005	Deprivation of Liberty Safeguards (DoLS) authorises the deprivation of a person's liberty (their 'detention') in a registered care home or hospital, where the care they need has to be provided in a manner which amounts to a deprivation of their liberty, and where the use of the Mental Health Act is not appropriate. The person concerned has to lack capacity to be eligible for the use of these powers	A standard authorisation can last for up to 12 months (dependent on the recommendation of the **best interest assessor (BIA)**) before a new assessment must take place
Community DoLS'	Where someone who lacks capacity and is being cared for in a way that amounts to a deprivation of their liberty, but outside of a registered care home or hospital (for example, in supported accommodation) the current process involves approaching the Court of Protection for a declaration	Time limits would be at the discretion of the Court, but annual reviews are generally a minimum expectation

CTOs and guardianship will be considered in more detail in Chapter 5. In this chapter, we will focus on the situations where compulsion relates to an admission to hospital.

Does the person meet the criteria for admission under the MHA?

Deciding whether or not someone meets the criteria for compulsory admission to hospital is similar to building a 'case' in court (see Figure 3.1). It isn't enough that someone has a mental disorder (including a mental illness like schizophrenia). You also need to make sure that all the building blocks are in place before you reach your decision.

This section will consider these criteria in detail.

Figure 3.1 Understanding the criteria in practice: s2, s3 and s4

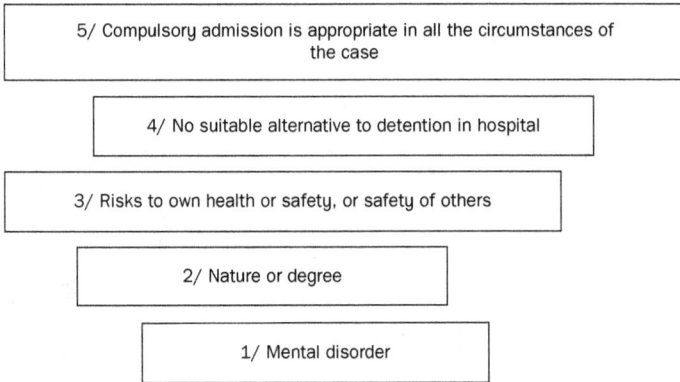

5/ Compulsory admission is appropriate in all the circumstances of the case

4/ No suitable alternative to detention in hospital

3/ Risks to own health or safety, or safety of others

2/ Nature or degree

1/ Mental disorder

Criteria 1: mental disorder

A '"mental disorder" means any disorder or disability of the mind; and "mentally disordered" shall be construed accordingly' (s1).

The person has a mental disorder: The requirement that a person has to have a mental disorder in order to be considered for the use of compulsion under the Act is common to all sections of the MHA. What should be considered as a mental disorder has the same simplified definition throughout the Act, except that there are additional conditions imposed on someone detained for treatment (or subject to guardianship) solely on the basis of their learning disability which *do not* apply to sections related to assessment (the learning disability 'qualification', see below).

The term 'mental disorder' therefore covers a wide range of mental disorders.

> ### Checklist: different sorts of mental disorder
>
> Clinically recognised conditions which could fall within the MHA's definition of a mental disorder (CoP figure 1 p26):
>
> ✓ affective disorders, such as depression and bipolar disorder
> ✓ schizophrenia and delusional disorders
> ✓ neurotic, stress-related and somatoform disorders, such as anxiety, phobic disorders, obsessive compulsive disorders, post-traumatic stress disorder and hypochondriacal disorders
> ✓ organic mental disorders such as dementia and delirium (however caused)
> ✓ personality and behavioural changes caused by brain injury or damage (however acquired)
> ✓ personality disorders
> ✓ mental and behavioural disorders caused by psychoactive substance use (but see section below concerning the exclusion)
> ✓ eating disorders, non-organic sleep disorders and non-organic sexual disorders
> ✓ learning disabilities (but see below under 'qualification')
> ✓ autistic spectrum disorders (including Asperger syndrome)
> ✓ behavioural and emotional disorders of children and adolescents
>
> (Note: this list is not exhaustive.)

However, there is one exclusion and one qualification to how the term 'mental disorder' should be understood. These are considered next.

The exclusion is that someone cannot be categorised as having a mental disorder within the meaning of the MHA *only* because they abuse drugs or alcohol – however, where drugs or alcohol result in a mental disorder, it is quite possible to use the Act to either assess or treat that disorder. An example of an assessment of a person with a drug or alcohol problem, which may be associated with a mental disorder follows.

> ### Example from practice
>
> Serge is picked up by the police, and taken to A&E under s136 of the MHA. He is paranoid, believing that sarin gas has been released onto the streets of the city in an attempt to kill him, because he used to belong to the Solidarity movement in Poland. He admits to taking a cocktail of street drugs, but won't say what, and becomes more agitated and aggressive when staff in A&E attempt to take a blood sample, believing that they are part of the conspiracy against him. He needs to be restrained by police officers and security staff.

When he is assessed by the AMHP and a doctor, he tells them about his certainty that there is a conspiracy against him. He also says he knows this is the case because all the staff in A&E are wearing uniform. This is why he knows he can trust the section 12 doctor and AMHP, as they are in 'normal' clothes. He wants to be admitted to a psychiatric ward where he thinks he will be safe from the FSB.

Although it is likely that his mental disorder is as a result of drug misuse, and will resolve itself, the assessors decide he should be admitted onto a psychiatric ward for further assessment, and that given his lack of capacity and unpredictable behaviour since being in A&E, this should be authorised by the use of s2.

The qualification: learning disability and the MHA

For the purposes of the Act, a 'learning disability' is defined as 'a state of arrested or incomplete development of the mind which includes significant impairment of intelligence and social functioning'.

CoP 20.4

The learning disability qualification in the MHA relates to people with a learning disability, where the only reason you wish to section them is because of their learning disability. This does not apply to s2 or s4 of the Act, only to s3 and other sections related to longer term care (s7 – guardianship) and treatment (i.e. s17A/CTO, 37, etc). You can therefore admit someone with a learning disability on s2 (or use a holding section like s5(2) or s136) without having to worry about whether or not their learning disability is also associated with *'abnormally aggressive or seriously irresponsible conduct'*.

Remember!

Having a learning disability that is not associated with 'abnormally aggressive or seriously irresponsible conduct' does not prevent someone with a learning disability being treated for a different sort of mental disorder, such as a mental illness under the MHA. In practice, most people with a learning disability who need to be compulsorily admitted to hospital are admitted for assessment or treatment for a mental illness, not because of their learning disability.

Therefore, when considering the use of s3, guardianship or CTO, solely on the basis that the person has a learning disability, that disability can only be considered as a mental disorder if it is associated with *abnormally aggressive or seriously irresponsible conduct*.

This learning disability qualification *does not apply* to the MCA. Because of this, people who cannot be detained under the MHA *may* be able to be detained under DoLS.

Autism, learning disability and the MHA

Someone with autism will not automatically fall into the learning disability (LD) category. This is because a learning disability is defined as having both 'a significant impairment of intelligence **and** social functioning'. Therefore, for someone without an 'impairment' of 'intelligence', but with the impairment of social functioning characterised by autism, they would not fit the LD definition in the Mental Health Act, and the LD 'qualification' would not apply.

Disorders of the mind vs disorders of the brain

Mental Disorder means any disorder of the mind. MHA s1(2)

Is unable to make a decision for himself in relation to the matter because of an impairment of, or disturbance in the functioning of the mind or brain.

MCA s2(1)

The Mental Health Act definition excludes conditions that are solely disorders of the brain, such as the effects of strokes, brain injury or minimally conscious states unless these result in a mental disorder. Such disorders do, however, fall within the definition used in the MCA for the deprivation of liberty safeguards.

Criteria 2: nature or degree

The mental disorder is of a nature or degree that warrants admission to hospital. To justify the use of compulsion under the MHA, the person's mental disorder must be of a nature or degree to warrant its use.

Nature refers to the *type* of mental disorder that is observed, how it manifests itself both from the point of view of the patient, and objectively what you see. It is also about the *pattern* of the disorder over time. This could be the basis on which someone who was well known to experience a decline in their mental state once they stopped taking medication might be assessed and detained on an s2 or s3 even in a situation where they are not yet 'acutely' unwell.

Degree is about the *intensity* with which a person experiences symptoms, and how the symptoms affect their lives. For example, a patient who is able to negotiate with their voices to leave them be until the end of the day so that they can finish important work would be unlikely to meet the criteria of 'degree', but a second patient, who feels compelled to act on the instructions from the voices that they hear, most probably would.

Example from practice

Joe's case – nature or degree?

When thinking about Joe's case, the AMHP and doctors looked back over his history as well as considering the current situation.

In terms of the current 'degree' of mental disorder, this was not currently an acute problem. He did appear to be hearing 'noises' or 'voices' and was prescribed Olanzapine, which he had stopped taking. Neither the doctors nor the AMHP felt he met the criteria in terms of the 'degree' of his disorder.

When making a judgement about the 'nature' of the mental disorder, they needed to think about how Joe's mental disorder affected him over time.

They considered Joe's impulsiveness, and the number of times he had been assaulted or had assaulted other people. They considered Joe's poor short- and long-term memory, and the difficulties he had in retaining information, and keeping to pre-arranged plans. They also considered the number of times he had stopped taking medication and become unwell.

The assessing team concluded that the *nature* of Joe's illness was such that it did warrant compulsory admission to hospital.

Criteria 3: compulsory admission is necessary in the interests of their health or their safety or the safety of others

It is only necessary to fulfil one of these areas of risk in order to meet this criteria.

Their *health*: This refers to both physical *and* mental health, so, for example where acute depression leads to a person's physical health deteriorating, this criteria would be fulfilled.

Their *safety*: This criteria relates to how the mental disorder affects/influences their ability to keep themselves safe. So a woman who tries to 'cut out' the bugs that she believes live beneath her skin could fulfil the criteria.

The *safety* of others: In a similar way to the criteria above, this relates to the way in which the mental disorder presents itself and may endanger the safety of others.

The following box gives details of the factors to be considered in the detention for a person's own health or safety from the CoP advice.

Factors to be considered in deciding whether patients should be detained for their own health or safety include:

* the evidence suggesting that patients are at risk of:
  o suicide
  o self-harm
  o self-neglect or being unable to look after their own health or safety

- o jeopardising their own health or safety accidentally, recklessly or unintentionally, or
- o that their mental disorder is otherwise putting their health or safety at risk
- any evidence suggesting that the patient's mental health will deteriorate if they do not receive treatment, including the views of the patient or carers, relatives or close friends (especially those living with the patient) about the likely course of the disorder
- patient's own skills and experience in managing their condition
- the patient's capacity to consent to or refuse admission and treatment (and the availability of the deprivation of liberty safeguards (DoLS))
- whether the patient objects to treatment for mental disorder – or is likely to
- the reliability of such evidence, including what is known of the history of the patient's mental disorder and the possibility of their condition improving
- the potential benefits of treatment, which should be weighed against any adverse effects that being detained might have on the patient's wellbeing, and whether other methods of managing the risk are available.

CoP 14.9

The CoP advice on the factors to be considered for the protection of others is as follows:

In considering whether detention is necessary for the protection of other people, the factors to consider are the nature of the risk to other people arising from the patient's mental disorder, the likelihood that harm will result and the severity of any potential harm, taking into account:

- that it is not always possible to differentiate risk of harm to the patient from the risk of harm to others
- the reliability of the available evidence, including any relevant details of the patient's clinical history and past behaviour, such as contact with other agencies and (where relevant) criminal convictions and cautions
- the willingness and ability of those who live with the patient and those who provide care and support to the patient to cope with and manage the risk, and
- whether other methods of managing the risk are available, and
- harm to other people includes psychological as well as physical harm.

CoP 14.10

Remember!

Evidence shows that there are particular risks where

- children or adults (especially adults who are less able to protect them-selves) become involved in someone else's delusional belief system;
- children or adults (especially adults who are less able to protect them-selves) become involved in someone else's suicide planning.

Example from practice

Jenny had two children, aged five and seven years. After the birth of a third child, she developed 'postpartum psychosis' which resulted in her becoming convinced that the new baby was possessed by a 'demon' and needed to be cleaned to exorcise it.

The health visitor became concerned that the baby was showing distress, and when she asked Jenny about the 'red' patches on the baby's skin, Jenny explained that she was using strong soap to try and 'clean out the devil'. The health visitor recognised the dangers to the child because the mother had included the child in her delusional belief system and made an urgent referral to children's and mental health services.

Criteria 4: no suitable alternatives to detention in hospital

s2 – the nature or degree of their disorder warrants detention in hospital for assessment (or assessment followed by treatment) for at least a limited period.

s3 – The nature or degree of their mental disorder make it appropriate that he receive medical treatment in hospital.... Such treatment cannot be provided unless he is detained.

Does the care need to be provided in hospital?

Both s2 and s3 emphasise that the need to be in hospital should relate to the nature or degree of the mental disorder (i.e. there should be a reason that relates to the person's mental disorder, why they need to be in hospital in order to receive the assessment or treatment they need). For s3 there is the added requirement that the person concerned should also not be willing to stay informally and take the necessary treatment. If there is no 'medical treatment' needed, the person cannot be detained.

This is one reason why it is important to understand MCA, as protections available under this Act may provide sufficient authority to assess or treat someone who lacks capacity.

Remember!

The MCA/DoLS may provide appropriate authority where:

- the service user lacks capacity to make relevant decisions;
- the focus of the admission to hospital is around care (for example, they are waiting for a residential placement to become available);
- they are not objecting to being in hospital or the treatment that they are expected to take;
- they are not expected to start to object to any psychiatric treatment that is needed;
- there is not a relevant and applicable advance decision to refuse necessary medical treatment, or someone with Lasting Power of Attorney objecting to admission or necessary treatment;
- the continued admission is in their best interests.

Is there an alternative, less restrictive way of providing the care that is needed?

In deciding whether it is necessary to detain patients, doctors and AMHPs must always consider the alternative ways of providing the treatment or care they need.

CoP 14.11

Again, awareness of the person's full circumstances is essential, as is the application of a social perspective to the situation.

Example from practice

Hilary has a delusional disorder, which manifests as a conviction that her daughter Hannah has been replaced by an alien. Hilary does, however, work full time in a shop, and while work and life are going well, these beliefs are in the background, and don't bother her (or her daughter) too much.

Hilary's husband makes contact, asking for a Mental Health Act assessment because Hilary is not able to work as usual due to pandemic restrictions and her delusions have become a lot worse and she isn't sleeping.

During the assessment, Hilary readily agrees that she believes her daughter has been replaced, and not sleeping is making things worse, but says she has made arrangements to start volunteering with a friend at a vaccination centre starting the following day. She also says she would like something to help her sleep, as long as it didn't interfere with her volunteering.

Both doctors want to make recommendations, which they do. However, Jamie the AMHP felt an alternative plan was possible. He made a plan with Hilary and her husband that Hilary would start to take sleeping tablets and continue with her volunteering, and Jamie would hold onto the recommendations, and continue to assess for the next two weeks to see whether the plan was working. After 10 days Jamie returned and confirmed with Hilary and her husband that things were improving. The recommendations were struck through with the words 'not required', much to Hilary's relief.

Informal admission is appropriate where:

- the service user needs assessment or treatment, and this cannot safely be provided in the community; and
- the service user has the capacity to make decisions about care and treatment, and is willing to agree to necessary restrictions that admission to a psychiatric ward would entail, as well as the assessment and treatment needed.

Informal admission won't be appropriate where:

- the service user has a history of changing their mind after admissions;
- the person objects to the assessment or treatment needed (even if they are happy to be admitted);
- The service user lacks capacity to agree to admission (even if they don't object to it).

Deprivation of Liberty: the impact on the Supreme Court ruling on decision-making in MHAs

The clarification by the Supreme Court in March 2014 that a 'deprivation of liberty' would occur where the person was '**under continuous supervision, and control, and not free to leave**' has had a significant impact on MHA decision-making. In effect, given that admission to a psychiatric ward will almost always entail a deprivation of liberty, informal admission is only possible if the person has capacity, understands the restrictions that will be necessary, and willingly accepts them.

Below are some examples from practice to illustrate the issues.

Example from practice

Maggie is 72. She lives alone with her dog and her cat, but acts as an informal carer for her brother who lives locally and has schizophrenia. She is familiar with mental health services as a result. In the last few months, following the death of two close friends, she has becoming increasingly depressed. She has lost weight and has started to have daily thoughts about ending her life. Today, she went with her dog Max to the local railway station and tried to jump in front of a train. She was brought into a place of safety under s136 of the Act.

When assessed, Maggie is able to acknowledge how depressed she is and that she is scared that she might hurt herself again. She wants to be somewhere safe, and says she is willing to take any medication recommended, and also stay on the ward until staff feel it is safe for her to leave.

Because the AMHP and doctor seeing her were satisfied that she understood what the decision to come into hospital would entail – i.e. being under supervision to keep herself safe, taking medication and not leaving until staff felt it was safe to do so – they were satisfied that she had the capacity to make the decision to come into hospital informally, even though the care she needed (because of the risks she presented to herself) would amount to a deprivation of her liberty.

Example from practice

Freddie is 28 years old, he has a diagnosis of bipolar disorder and is currently very 'high'. He has grandiose beliefs that he has cured himself of the bipolar through the use of 'special intellectual powers' and wants the chance to enable others to be cured by him. His girlfriend is concerned that he has recently bought three sports cars and is being contacted daily by fraudsters offering to invest money for him abroad. He stopped taking lithium three months ago after a bad reaction with other medication.

When seen by the assessing team, they express their concern for his welfare, and his mood, and suggest an admission to hospital for treatment to re-establish his medication. Freddie poo-poos the idea that he needs medication, but is keen on the idea of coming into hospital, as this will allow him to 'cure' many more people with his powers.

Although Freddie is agreeing to come into hospital, this is not a decision made with capacity. He does not believe he has a mental disorder which needs treatment, and therefore would not accept medication willingly. Using the four-step test, (see p. 8) although he can take in and remember the information being provided about the decision (to come into hospital for treatment) he is unable to 'use' it to balance up the pros and cons of the decision, because he does not believe it. The bipolar disorder is interfering within his decision-making ability and he therefore does not have the capacity to make the decision.

> Because the AMHP and doctors are aware that once on the ward he would be deprived of his liberty, they therefore use the legal framework of the Mental Health Act to authorise this deprivation and ensure he gets the treatment that he requires for the mental disorder.

For s3, the following criteria must also be fulfilled:

> Appropriate medical treatment is available to him.
>
> MHA s3(2)(d)

> The appropriate medical treatment test must be applied to ensure that no one is detained (or remains detained) for treatment, or is on a CTO, unless medical treatment for their mental disorder is both appropriate and available.
>
> CoP 23.8

This criteria applies to sections where treatment of a mental disorder is the main purpose of the use of compulsion (e.g. for s3 or CTO). Although the 'appropriate treatment' does not need to be perfect, it does need to be appropriate to the mental disorder, and the particular needs of the individual patient. The Code also tells us what we should consider when we think about 'all other circumstances' that may affect the decision about whether treatment is 'appropriate' for a particular person.

> The other circumstances of a patient's case might, for example, include factors such as:
>
> - the patient's physical health – how this might impact on the effectiveness of the available medical treatment for the patient's mental disorder and the impact that the treatment might have in return
> - the patient's age
> - any physical disabilities or sensory impairments the patient has
> - the patient's culture and ethnicity
> - the patient's gender, gender identity, sexual identity and sexual orientation
> - the patient's religion or beliefs
> - the location of the available treatment
> - the implications of the treatment for the patient's family and social relationships, including their role as a parent (where applicable)
> - its implications for the patient's education or work
> - the consequences for the patient, and other people, if the patient does not receive the treatment available (for mentally disordered offenders

about to be sentenced for an offence, the consequence will sometimes be a prison sentence), and

- the patient's views and wishes about what treatment works for them and what doesn't.

CoP 23.12

Example from practice

Kerry is 15 years old and has anorexia. She is treated as an outpatient for some time. When her weight falls below a minimum safe level, she is admitted on an s2, and then an s3. However, when she appeals against her section, Kerry does so in the basis that the treatment in a specialist unit is not 'suitable' for her needs, because it is many miles from home and has cut her off from her friends, family and her school. The MHRT agrees and tells the RC to consider using a CTO so that Kerry can return home, but with the safety net of being able to be recalled to hospital if her weight falls dangerously low.

Treatment or detention?

Just detaining someone in hospital without offering treatment would be unlikely to meet the criteria for this test, unless it can be demonstrated that the care that they receive does amount to treatment (CoP 23.18). There are two aspects to the definition of treatment:

1 the meaning of medical treatment;
2 the purpose of medical treatment.

The meaning of medical treatment is defined by the MHA as follows:

'medical treatment' includes nursing, psychological intervention and special-ist mental health habilitation, rehabilitation and care (but see also subsection (4) below);

MHA s145

The purpose of medical treatment is defined as follows:

Any reference in this Act to medical treatment, in relation to mental disorder, shall be construed as a reference to medical treatment the purpose of which is to alleviate, or prevent a worsening of, the disorder or one or more of its symptoms or manifestations.

MHA s145(4)

As you can see, the definition of medical treatment is very broad but it is qualified further by subsection 4, which focuses on the purpose of the medical treatment.

This means that the treatment envisaged must relate to the mental disorder the person is suffering from, and have a 'purpose' of alleviating or preventing a worsening of that disorder.

'Purpose' is an important word, as it means that you don't have to be able to prove that a particular intervention will be successful, but your intention should be that it should.

> In order to be deemed appropriate, medical treatment must be for the purpose of alleviating or preventing a worsening of the patient's mental disorder or its symptoms or manifestations. It must also be appropriate, having taken account of the nature and degree of the patient's mental disorder and all their particular circumstances, including cultural, ethnic and religious or belief considerations.
>
> CoP 23.9

Criteria 5: admission is appropriate in all the circumstances of the case

Has the AMHP considered all other relevant factors?

> 1 (A) **If that professional (the *AMHP*) is –**
>   (a) satisfied that such an application ought to be made in respect of the patient; and
>   (b) of the opinion, having regard to any wishes expressed by relatives of the patient or any other relevant circumstances, that it is necessary or proper for the application to be made by him, he shall make the application.
>
> 2 Before making an application for the admission of a patient to hospital an approved mental health professional shall interview the patient in a suitable manner and *satisfy himself that detention in a hospital is in all the circumstances of the case the most appropriate way of providing the care and medical treatment of which the patient stands in need.*
>
> MHA s13

The criteria above are specific to the role of the AMHP – in other words even if a service user fulfils all the other criteria for the use of a section of the Act, the AMHP is still obliged to gather information from a number of sources, including the nearest relative, other relatives and the service user themselves, and 'satisfy' themselves that detention in hospital (or the use of guardianship or a CTO) is in all the circumstances of the case the 'most appropriate way of providing the care and medical treatment'.

Therefore, even if a person does appear to meet the criteria of the Act, including in situations where you have doctors who have made, or wish to make medical recommendations, there is no obligation on the AMHP to make an application if they do not judge that it is appropriate to do so.

However, once you have made a decision that admission is appropriate, you have an obligation to make an application (or using the words of the Act, the AMHP 'shall' make an application).

Considering what 'appropriate' means in practice

In this section, we focus on what 'appropriate' might mean and the wider factors you need to consider when deciding whether to make an application or not.

The first of these key tasks for the AMHP is to look at the wider 'social' situation of the patient and decide whether given everything you know about a particular patient, they should or should not be admitted formally to hospital. In order to do so, *all* AMHPs need to be culturally competent and have the necessary skills, knowledge and understanding relating to the cultural impact of assessments in order to undertake this successfully.

Checklist: cultural competence

Keep the following points in mind:

✓ Culture is specific to each person, so it is not enough to have a general understanding of the 'social norms' of a particular social group; it is also important to understand (as far as possible) how the individual and their family experiences that culture.

✓ A key issue is whether the behaviour and presentation of the person is significantly different from others from the same culture.

✓ It is very important not to presume behaviour 'must' be culturally appropriate, or that it is not without exploring these issues.

✓ Asking questions about 'difference', both in terms of what people who know the person well would understand as their 'normal' behaviour, and how this has changed or caused concern, can be very helpful.

The Code of Practice suggests a number of other factors that need to be taken into account when considering the use of compulsion:

In all cases, consideration must be given to:

• the patient's wishes and view of their own needs
• the patient's age and physical health
• any past wishes or feelings expressed by the patient

- the patient's cultural background
- the patient's social and family circumstances
- the impact that any future deterioration or lack of improvement in the patient's condition would have on their children, other relatives or carers, especially those living with the patient, including an assessment of these people's ability and willingness to cope, and
- the effect on the patient, and those close to the patient, of a decision to admit or not to admit under the Act.

CoP 14.8

Considering the use of the MCA, or the person's own capacity and willingness to accept assessment or treatment informally is an essential part of the process. This is considered more in the section below on making decisions.

Choosing between sections and between acts

Choosing between sections of the MHA

Paragraphs 14.26–29 of the MHA Code of Practice provide AMHPs and doctors with guidance when making decisions about whether s2 or s3 would be more appropriate.

Section 2 should only be used if:

- the full extent of the nature and degree of a patient's condition is unclear
- there is a need to carry out an initial in-patient assessment in order to formulate a treatment plan, or to reach a judgement about whether the patient will accept treatment on a voluntary basis following admission, or
- there is a need to carry out a new in-patient assessment in order to re-formulate a treatment plan, or to reach a judgement about whether the patient will accept treatment on a voluntary basis.

CoP 14.27

Remember!

Should s2 always be the section of choice when first admitting a person to hospital, regardless of their previous care or treatment in the community? Strong views exist on this subject on both sides! Given the legal status of the Code of Practice, all AMHPs *must* follow its advice, unless they have a good reason not to. Unless case law suggests the interpretation in the Code is inappropriate, it is one we have an obligation to follow.

The current version of the Code has inserted the word 'only' into advice on when to use s2. The impact of this is that it limits when s2 is used, and opens up the possibility that s3 should be used in situations where a reassessment isn't needed, but a restart of medication is required.

> Section 3 should be used if:
>
> - the patient is already detained under section 2 (detention under section 2 cannot be renewed by a new section 2 application), or
> - the nature and current degree of the patient's mental disorder, the essential elements of the treatment plan to be followed and the likelihood of the patient accepting treatment on a voluntary basis are already sufficiently established to make it unnecessary to undertake a new assessment under section 2.
>
> CoP 14.28

The following quotes describe situations where you cannot use s2.

> The powers under section 2 can only be used for the limited purpose for which they were intended. They cannot be used to further detain patients for the purposes of assessment beyond the 28 days period. Nor can they be used as a temporary alternative to detention under section 3 merely to allow an application to be made to the county court under section 29 for an order to appoint an acting nearest relative ...
>
> Mental Health Act Reference Guide 8.11

So, to reiterate:

1 Section 2 cannot be used to detain someone *already* on s2.
2 Section 2 should not be used to *avoid the objection* of a nearest relative who opposes the use of s3.

If you wanted to use s2 in a situation where you were aware that the nearest relative would be likely to object to the use of an s3, it is important to be clear how the person fits the criteria for s2 rather than justifying the use of s2 on the basis that the nearest relative was objecting to s3.

> ## Remember!
>
> If you are in a situation where you need to admit someone on an s2 against the strong objections of the nearest relative, maintain contact with that relative, continuing to discuss their concerns and potential objections if s3

becomes necessary. In this way you will have a clear idea about whether you believe their objection is reasonable, or whether it would be appropriate to make an application for displacement to the courts for that or other reasons.

Table 3.3 provides examples explaining the criteria further.

Deciding between the MHA and the DoLS

The MHA should be used in cases where the assessment or treatment needed is for a mental disorder, and the person objects to what is suggested (either at the time of admission, or via an advance decision or someone with a relevant LPA), or is likely to in the near future based on the nature of their illness and their past history, or they lack capacity to agree to admission and essential elements of

Table 3.3 S2 and s3 criteria and examples

s2	s3
not a known patient	well known to team or service (doesn't have to be personal knowledge, can be recorded knowledge)
no clear diagnosis or treatment plan	
a well-known patient with a different presentation	
	revolving-door patient
less likely to have recent admissions or where it isn't clear whether the person will start to agree to treatment on a voluntary basis once admitted	established treatment plan
	clear and established pattern of 'illness' and relapse history
Examples	
s2 Farrah has an established diagnosis of having a learning disability. He is 16 years old, and his behaviour is becoming more difficult to manage in the community, because of its increasingly sexualised content. He has come to the attention of the police as result. A specialist placement is found for him, but the placement is keen that he be admitted on an s3 as his learning disability is established. However, because Farrah has never been admitted before, and it is unclear whether the behavioural management approach in the ward will be helpful, the AMHP and his community RC successfully argue that he should be admitted under s2 for assessment, so that the suitability of the placement can be assessed, and a treatment plan developed.	**s3** Peter is 36 years old, has a diagnosis of paranoid schizophrenia and is regarded as a 'revolving-door' client. He has never believed he is unwell, or needs medication, and has always stopped taking it as soon as he was discharged from section. He has been occasionally picked up on an s136 but is often assessed in his own home.
	He has been assessed and placed on an s3 because, 1) he had a well-known diagnosis; 2) he had a well-established treatment plan; and 3) it was not likely (from past experience) that he would ever agree to taking medication on a voluntary basis.

the care plan, and the admission would amount to a deprivation of their liberty. It should also be considered where the risks are primarily to others, or where the person is under 16 years, and parental authority is insufficient for some reason.

The DoLS should be seen as the appropriate option in other cases where *care* needs to be provided to an incapacitated person in a manner that is equivalent to detention and the MHA is not appropriate. For example, it may be appropriate where a patient who lacks capacity is only remaining on a ward while a suitable community placement is found, and they are happy to receive treatment recommended to them (see MHA CoP page 112 for an example) Another common scenario could be where a person with a mental disorder lacks capacity and needs admission to a general hospital for physical health treatment. In other words, their admission is not related to assessment or treatment for their mental health – it is their physical health that is causing concern.

It should be remembered that the DoLS procedures only authorise detention not necessary treatment or care. Any treatment needed must be provided either with consent or relying on best interests and the protections of s5 of the MCA.

In most cases, a person needing admission for assessment or treatment of a mental disorder who is resisting admission will need to be admitted using the MHA.

Summary

- In order to be subject to the MHA, a person must have a 'mental disorder' of a nature or degree which warrants the use of the Act.
- 'Mental disorder' has a very wide meaning, but excludes situations where a person's problems are only related to substance misuse. However, people with mental health problems caused by substance misuse may be able to be detained under the Act.
- There are restrictions that relate to the longer use of the Act with someone with a learning disability, unless they also have another mental disorder.
- There has to be evidence of risks to the person, their health, or other people in order to justify the use of compulsion.
- Alternatives to admissions must always be considered, and the AMHP must be satisfied that it is 'appropriate' to use the powers of the Act.
- If the admission is likely to lead to a deprivation of their liberty, the person must either have sufficient capacity to agree to the plan, or if they disagree (or lack capacity to agree) another source of authority such as the MHA will be needed.
- AMHPs have a responsibility for coordinating the assessment, and making sure they are able to assess the patient in an 'appropriate manner'. This might include making sure an advocate or interpreter is present, or using powers under s135 to remove a patient to a place of safety prior to completing an assessment under the MHA.
- Even if the person meets all the 'medical' criteria for admission, the AMHP is still obliged to consider 'all the circumstances of the case' before deciding whether to make an application.

4 Implementing decisions and admission to hospital

In order for AMHPs and other professionals to implement decisions and effect admission to hospital under the MHA we need to have an understanding of both our own roles and responsibilities and those of our colleagues who work in partner agencies.

By the end of the chapter, you should have an understanding of:

- Who to inform about the outcome of the assessment
- What to do when you decide not to admit a patient to hospital
- Arrangements for the transport ('conveyance') of patients to hospital
- Time limits in respect of making applications
- Procedure for checking that a medical recommendation is valid
- Procedure for making the application
- Law on admission to hospital on the basis of an application
- Practice issues relating to the AMHP Outline Report and Full Report
- Patient Rights under Section 132

Implementing decisions

Telling people about your decision

Clearly, the most important person to tell is the person you have accessed. Remember, you should also be letting them know about their rights if you have decided to detain them. These include:

- the right to appeal to hospital managers and independent tribunal;
- the right to free legal representation (for the MHRT);
- the right to support from an IMHA.

But other people you need to think about include:

- the ward the patient is going to (to ensure they are still expected, and to pass on essential information);

- the nearest relative and other key supporters (subject to rules around confidentiality);
- professionals involved in that person's care, such as their GP, assessing doctors and care coordinator.

Example from practice

Ellie normally has a good relationship with her family, but when unwell becomes very paranoid and suspicious of them. In other words, she loses capacity to decide what information should be shared with them, because her paranoia gets in the way of her ability to use the information about whether her family should be told what is happening to her.

Ellie's social worker encourages her to develop a crisis plan, so that when she is unwell, and insisting her family not be told anything, professionals have access to information about her wishes. When a crisis next occurs and Ellie is admitted using the MHA, the AMHP (once satisfied that she does currently lack capacity to make the decision) can make an informed decision that it would be in Ellie's best interests to tell her family what is happening, as her crisis plan states that this is what she would have wanted to happen, had she had capacity for that decision.

What to do when you decide not to admit the person

There is no obligation on an AMHP or nearest relative to make an application for admission just because the statutory criteria are met.

CoP 14.103

Where AMHPs decide not to apply for a patient's detention they should record the reasons for their decision. The decision should be supported, where necessary, by an alternative framework of care or treatment (or both). AMHPs should decide how to pursue any actions which their assessment indicates are necessary to meet the needs of the patient. That might include, for example, referring the patient to social, health or other services.

CoP 14.104

Of course, there will be many occasions when you decide not to admit a person to hospital – and it is important to remember that your role as an AMHP does not 'stop' where you decide admission isn't necessary. You need also to decide what other plans may be have to be made to support the patient. Such plans could include:

- the patient working with the crisis team;
- the patient coming into a crisis house, or deciding to stay temporarily with a friend or relative;

- the AMHP and doctors deciding to use guardianship to support the person in the community;
- the AMHP recommending that although the use of the MHA isn't indicated, the person is being detained and so the use of the DoL Safeguards should be considered.

Example from practice

Mohammed has schizophrenia. He is usually supported at home by a combination of family members, a community psychiatric nurse (CPN) and his GP. Last week he was admitted to hospital with pneumonia. He has continued to accept his depot, but today wanted to leave the hospital due to long-standing delusional beliefs that he was about to marry into the Royal Family. Section 5(2) was used, and an MHA assessment requested. The assessing team decided Mohammed did not need assessment or treatment under the MHA, but lacked capacity to understand that he did need to stay in hospital to complete his treatment for pneumonia. They therefore recommended that the ward /hospital issue themselves with an urgent authorisation under the DoLS processes, and ask for a standard authorisation at the same time.

Deciding you need more time

Most compulsory admissions require prompt action. Applicants have up to 14 days (depending on when the patient was last examined by a doctor as part of the assessment) in which to decide whether to make the application, starting with the day they personally last saw the patient. There may be cases where AMHPs conclude that they should delay taking a final decision in order to see whether the patient's condition changes, or whether successful alternatives to detention can be put in place in the interim.

CoP 14.87

There is also the option open to the AMHP of deciding you need more time before making a final decision. This could happen, for example, where doctors have made recommendations, but the patient and their family want to try a community plan first. In this situation, you could decide to keep the recommendations, but delay your own decision until you are confident that the community plan is working. AMHPs have 14 days from the time that the second medical recommendation was made in which to make their decision.

However, it is important to remember if you decide to do this that it remains your responsibility to make a final decision, one way or another. This shouldn't be delegated to a different AMHP (as they were not part of the original decision-making process).

What to do when you can't admit because there isn't a bed available

This is happening more and more – and each area has their own processes to help AMHPs and other mental health staff manage until admission is possible. However, here are some of the options available:

- Always alert a more senior member of staff (such as your AMHP lead) about the situation. They can help you decide what to do next.
- Be clear about the risks involved, who is at risk and what the consequences might be for different people. Pass this information on to those responsible for locating a suitable bed.
- Think about whether it is possible to develop a crisis plan with the person, their family/supporters and other professionals to keep the person safe until a bed is located.
- Consider whether you can use your local s140 policy to admit the person – is this a case that constitutes 'special urgency'?
- If the person is in A&E or a health-based place of safety, it is the responsibility of staff there to keep the person safe until a bed has been located. Make arrangements so that staff know how to get hold of you, so that you can return or make an online application (presuming the person's mental health has remained disturbed, and you are happy to do this) when a bed becomes available.
- If you won't be available, make clear what the arrangement will be for staff to access an AMHP to complete an assessment.

> *The inability to admit a person in mental health crisis due to a lack of resources such as suitable beds should be seen as a serious issue, and indicates a commissioning failure that the local ICB (Integrated Care Board) should be made aware of. S140 places a legal duty on ICBs to identify places which will receive a person in cases of 'special urgency' as a result of their mental health. All areas should collect data and have systems in place to escalate problems to ICBs and Safeguarding Boards (amongst others) to resolve.*

Letting the nearest relative know about their right to mark an application

It is also important to remember that the nearest relative has the right to apply for admission as well as the AMHP. Therefore in situations where you have two medical recommendations, but decide it is not appropriate to make an application, you should be telling the nearest relative of their right to make an application.

Also, remember if you are assessing someone because their nearest relative has asked you to, and you decide not to admit, you must write to the nearest relative explaining your decision.

> # Remember!
>
> AMHPs and Doctors must interview the person face to face before making recommendations or applications

Getting the papers right

Medical recommendations

This section has been designed to help you 'spot' common errors on MHA medical recommendations for s2, s3 and s4. Section 2 is used as the main example. Where there is a variation from the requirements for s2, the variation and section number is specified.

When making medical recommendations, doctors have the choice of either using separate recommendations if they assessed separately, or a joint recommendation if they assessed together.

Separate or joint applications. Only use a joint application form when both doctors assess together, and you know you have a bed to admit the patient to. If you don't have a bed, or may need to pass on the assessment to another AMHP to complete, it would be better to use separate, single recommendations, so that the assessing AMHP has the choice of assessing again with another doctor, rather than assessing alone.

Legibility. The form must be legible and preferably completed using black ink.

Full name and address of the medical practitioner. The full name and address of the medical practitioner should be stated. Initials are not adequate. The address should be their full professional address (i.e. the place where they work) and should include the name of the town and postcode.

Full name and address of the patient. The full name and address of the patient should be stated. Both recommendations must carry the same name and address, again using the full name and postal address. If you are not sure about the name, as long as both recommendations and application use the same details, this will be sufficient.

Date of most recent examination. The doctor must examine the patient face to face. No more than five full days can elapse between the two medical examinations. The date of the examination must be on or before the date of signing the recommendation, i.e. the doctor can assess the patient one day and sign the recommendation the following day.

Qualifications. To qualify for making a recommendation, both doctors must be fully registered with the General Medical Council (GMC). Check that at least one of the doctors has indicated that they are s12 approved on the form. Whenever possible, the other doctor should either have prior acquaintance with the patient or also be approved under section 12. Strike out whichever does not apply. (Section 4 only – i.e. in an emergency – the recommendation may be made by any fully registered doctor, regardless of whether they are section 12 approved, or previously knew the patient.)

> ### Remember!
>
> At least one of the two doctors must be s12 approved (i.e. a psychiatrist) and they must have personally seen the patient no more than five days apart. In an emergency, (for s4) any registered doctor can make a recommendation.

Patient at risk to self or others. Delete the statements that are not applicable. The two recommendations do not have to agree with each other about type of risk.

Section 2 only – description of mental disorder and reason for use of detention. Describe the patient's symptoms and behaviour, and how they relate to the view that they have a mental disorder. Also the doctor should state why it is necessary to detain the patient, and why other options (including informal admission) are not suitable.

Section 3 only – treatment in hospital. State the reasons as to why the patient should receive treatment in hospital. Such reasons should include whether other methods of care or treatment (e.g. outpatient treatment or community services) are available and, if so, why they are not appropriate.

Section 3 only – description of clinical state. This should include the patient's behaviour, the presence of particular signs or symptoms and aspects of risk to support the condition identified above. It isn't enough just to state that the person has a particular diagnosis – doctors need to state what it is about the nature or degree of the mental disorder which means admission is appropriate.

Section 3 – state reasons why informal admission isn't possible. State the reasons as to why such treatment cannot be provided unless the patient is detained under section 3 of the Act. Reasons should indicate whether other methods of care or treatment (e.g. out-patient treatment or LSSA services) are available and if so why they are not appropriate, and why informal admission is not appropriate.

Section 3 only – availability of treatment. Doctors must complete the statement, 'I am of the opinion that, taking into account the nature and degree of the mental disorder from which the patient is suffering and all the other circumstances of the case, appropriate medical treatment is available to the patient at the following hospital (or one of the following hospitals) ...

[Enter name of hospital(s). If appropriate treatment is available only in a particular part of the hospital, say which part.]'

> ### Remember!
>
> You must write the name and address of the hospital – it is not possible to write only the name of the Trust involved. However, more than one hospital site could be recorded on the form.

You may name a specific ward on a specific hospital base (for example a psychiatric intensive care unit ward, if that is needed) or you may write the names of any possible hospitals the patient could be admitted to, as long as you are clear that the treatment needed would be available there.

Section 4 only. The reasons why a delay would be unjustifiable must be stated. This must not be solely on the grounds of convenience (e.g. the second doctor would prefer to see the patient in hospital) but on the grounds of immediate harm (i.e. less time than it would take to obtain the second medical recommendation) to the patient or others. Take care to delete the appropriate parts relating to when you were made aware of the problem.

Make sure the doctor has signed the recommendation! A medical recommendation that is unsigned is not valid and cannot be corrected later.

> ### Remember!
>
> Getting the medical recommendation forms right demonstrates an awareness of the importance of recommending the removal of a person's liberty, as well as avoiding the inconvenience of being called back to make amendments.

It is the AMHP's role to organise suitable doctors to examine the patient and complete any necessary recommendations. The AMHP has discretion to ask for a further medical examination of the patient if they are concerned about the quality of one or both of the recommendations. In circumstances where you are unsure about whether the doctors meet the requirements of the conflict of interest regulations (for example, both assessors were organised by a private hospital), or where it isn't possible to talk to one or both doctors about their reasons for making the recommendations, alternative assessors may well be justifiable. However, if you do this you must justify it in your report!

> ### Checklist: recommendations
>
> Completing forms:
>
> ✓ Know your own work address
> ✓ Check the patient's full name
> ✓ Check the patient's address with patient/family/carer/police, etc.
> ✓ Make sure the patient's name and address are the same on all forms

✓ Avoid postcodes unless you are accurate
✓ Complete the statements and give valid reasons

Most frequent errors:

✓ Omission of doctor's name and/or address, particularly on joint recommendations
✓ Incorrect dates
✓ Omission of patient's name and/or address

Invalidation:

✓ No signature
✓ Doctor not qualified or not registered with the GMC
✓ AMHP not qualified or not registered with their professional regulator
✓ Doctors or AMHP do not comply with the conflict of interest regulations
✓ Dates outside the legal limits (i.e. more than five days apart)

Checklist: section 2 and section 3 applications

✓ Full name and address of the admitting hospital
✓ Applicant's name and address in the correct boxes
✓ Name of LSSA the AMHP is approved by *and* (if different) the name of the authority the AMHP is undertaking the assessment on behalf of
✓ Patient's name in the correct box and exactly the same as on the other forms
✓ Patient's address details are correct and exactly the same as on the other forms
✓ Name and address of nearest relative or authorised person
✓ Has this person been consulted? If not why not?
✓ Date the patient was last seen by the applicant
✓ Applicant must comply with the conflict of interest regulations
✓ Reasons given in the instance of both doctors making a medical recommendation without prior acquaintance of the patient

Invalidation of applications

A document cannot be regarded as a proper application or recommendation if, for example:

• an application is not accompanied by the correct number of medical recommendations

- the application and the recommendations do not all relate to the same patient
- an application or recommendation is not signed at all, or is signed by someone not qualified to do so, or
- an application does not specify the correct hospital.

Reference Guide 8.90

In addition, if those making recommendations are in contravention of the conflict of interest regulations, the recommendations or application could not be relied upon.

Example from practice

Errol is a practice nurse in a GP surgery. He also has a bipolar disorder. He becomes unwell at work, and the lead GP in the practice makes one of the recommendations. However, because Errol is employed by the GP, this recommendation is in contravention of the conflict of interest regs, and has to be discarded.

Table 4.1 provides a quick checklist of the time limits for recommendations and applications for s2, s3 and s4.

Table 4.1   Time limits: quick check

Section 2 and Section 3		
Number of days	**Action**	
01	**Examination by first doctor**	There must be no more than five days between the two medical examinations
02		The applicant must have seen the patient within 14 days of the second medical recommendation
03		
04		
05		
06		
07	**Examination by second doctor**	
08		In theory, the applicant could have last seen the patient 13 days after the date of last medical examination and medical recommendation for admission. (However, this would not be good practice!)
09		
10		
11		

Section 2 and Section 3		
Number of days	Action	
12		
13		
14		
15		
16		
17		
18		
19		
20	**Admission must be before 23.59 hours on the twentieth day**	
Section 2 and Section 3		
Not more than five days may elapse between the dates of the two medical examinations		
Not more than 14 days may elapse between the applicant seeing the patient and signing the application		
The date of signing the application must be on or after the date of signing both medical recommendations		
The admission must be effected within 14 days of the date of the second medical examination		
Section 4		
Not more than 24 hours may elapse between medical examination and admission		
Not more than 24 hours may elapse between the applicant seeing the patient and signing the application		

Implementing decisions: conveyance to hospital

And now the process gets really difficult! The process of conveyance and admission to hospital is an area where the AMHP is potentially liable for a number of things. It is the AMHP who is responsible for the coordination of assessments under the Act and it is the AMHP who is responsible for the lawful conveyance of patients to hospital.

> ## Remember!
>
> - Consult and liaise with staff from other agencies, such as the police and ambulance services.
> - Establish the most appropriate conveyance arrangements.
> - Put together and record a management plan based on identified risks in relation to the conveyance of the patient to hospital.
> - Share the risk assessment with the ambulance service, police and other colleagues.

Roles and responsibilities: the AMHP

The AMHP is empowered to take the lead in all matters relating to conveyance to hospital of patients who are *liable to be detained* under the MHA. The AMHP is responsible for coordinating the entire process.

> ## Remember!
>
> If you are travelling separately, it would be useful to formally delegate the authority to convey, and ensure that the delegated person has the signed legal papers. This should be in writing and handed to ambulance staff.

Where the AMHP is the applicant, they have a duty to ensure that all necessary arrangements are made for the patient to be conveyed to hospital. How you access transportation varies across the country, so it is important when new to an area to find out the processes.

Options include:

- booking via the local ambulance service;
- booking via a private contractor;
- booking ahead vs booking once the assessment is complete.

Even where a bed has been arranged in advance, it is a good idea to ring and double-check that the ward is expecting you before signing the papers. You can also use this call to pass on any relevant information about the patient's presentation and needs (for example, whether they might need 1:1 nursing) and ensure you have the correct address for the admitting hospital. Also remember to give them your phone number – just in case they need to get back to you.

Delegating the conveyance

The AMHP is able to delegate the task of conveying the patient to another person, such as personnel from the ambulance service or the police. It is good practice and generally expected that the AMHP, or their delegated nominee, will accompany the patient to hospital, however, this is not always possible. There are some things to remember if you do delegate the authority to convey:

- The AMHP retains ultimate responsibility to ensure that the patient is conveyed in a lawful, safe and humane manner.
- If the AMHP delegates the conveyance of the patient they must be confident that the person accepting this responsibility is competent and fully aware of their responsibilities in relation to this task.
- Where there are delays in arranging admission, it may be necessary for the AMHP to delegate the task of coordinating conveyance to hospital staff (for example, staff in A&E, or MH liaison staff). If the task is delegated, make sure that a written form of authorisation is made available to the person who will be undertaking the conveyance.
- If the AMHP is unable to travel to the hospital, they should ensure that the ward is aware of this, and make sure those conveying have access to their contact details (or those of a manager, for example) in case problems arise later.

Remember!

The first doctor to see the patient when they get to the ward is likely to be very junior – so providing as much risk and other information as possible is essential. Consider asking the assessing doctors to complete a management plan for the ward (see appendix 2 for an example).

The AMHP should make sure if they are not going to the hospital with the patient that the ward have at least a verbal account of why the patient has been detained – ideally a brief report (as a minimum) should accompany the patient. In addition, it is useful to have a short written report from one of the doctors, explaining their views on the patient's mental health, and any advice on risks and how to manage them based on their observations and the information available to them during the admission.

Deciding how to manage the conveyance

The AMHP should take into account the needs of the patient and the views of the NR, friends, family, ambulance service or the police when deciding whether to accompany the patient to hospital in the same vehicle. They should also discuss any issues with the assessing doctors and consider their views. A decision should be reached by negotiation with the above, depending on individual circumstances.

If the patient would prefer to be accompanied by another professional or by any other adult, that person may be asked to escort the patient provided the AMHP is satisfied that this will not increase the risk of harm to the patient or to others and will not lead to undesirable delay.

It is for clinical commissioning groups (CCGs) to commission ambulance and patient transport services to meet the needs of people living in their areas. This includes services for transporting patients to and from hospital (and other places) under the Act.

CoP 17.22

Policies should ensure that AMHPs (in particular) are not left to negotiate arrangements with providers of transport services on an ad hoc basis, in the absence of clear expectations about the responsibilities of all those involved.

CoP 17.27

It is generally accepted that unless it is too dangerous to do so (in which case a police vehicle could be considered) an ambulance will in most cases be the most appropriate way to transport a patient to hospital after an MHA assessment.

However, it doesn't need to be a 'fully fledged' ambulance – different services can be commissioned as long as:

- the vehicle used is suitable for the purpose;
- suitably trained staff are available to support the patient – especially if they are sedated prior to the admission (in which case a health professional with suitable skills and training must accompany the patient – in most cases this will be a nurse);
- the type of transport would not negatively impact on the patient, or the views of community in which they live, and to whom they will return;
- the service is available in a timely manner.

Where a privately funded patient is requesting admission to a particular private hospital, the managers of that hospital are responsible for arranging the transport.

CoP 17.24

When to provide an escort

An escort will need to be provided in the following circumstances:

- if the patient is sedated, an appropriately trained medical professional must accompany them;
- if the patient or the transport service personnel would benefit from additional support;
- where the presence of a particular escort, e.g. relative, friend, nurse, social worker, is likely to be of benefit during the patient's conveyance to hospital;
- where the presence of the police is needed to prevent a breach of the peace or because the patient presents a physical risk to self or others.

The escort doesn't need to be the AMHP, but should be someone the AMHP feels is suitable for the task. A friend or relative cannot, however, 'insist' on accompanying the patient. Ultimately, it is up to the AMHP and the person in charge of the vehicle to decide who should provide an escort, and that decision should be based on any potential risks.

Timing

Depending on local commissioning arrangements, it may be possible that the ambulance will be available to transport the patient to hospital as soon as the assessment finishes. However, you may be in an area where an ambulance can only be booked after an assessment has finished and the receiving hospital identified. If this is the case, take account of this in your planning and consider the following:

* Who will be left with you in the property with the patient? Will the police, NR or doctors stay? If they won't stay, consider the risks of remaining in the house on your own, and feel free to ask for backup or insist on someone staying if you don't feel it is safe.
* You could also consider going and waiting outside – for example in a car – if you feel your presence is likely to exacerbate the situation. However, also consider the risks to the patient and others in the property when you make this decision.
* Make a note of the call log number when you talk to ambulance control, so that if the situation deteriorates or you need to check on when to expect the ambulance, you are able to contact the services quickly.

You can also upgrade an 'urgent' response to an 'immediate' response, and should consider this in the following circumstances:

* The patient's mental state deteriorates.
* Ambulance control are unable to meet the agreed time frame for hospital arrival and the AMHP does not agree to extend the time frame because of the patient's mental condition.

In such circumstances, the AMHP should not, as an initial response, telephone 999 but should contact ambulance control in the usual way and renegotiate the referral request and its response status. This may include the re-grading of the response to 'immediate' where the situation has deteriorated and the AMHP's assessment indicates a 999 response.

Due to the complexity of some of the journeys, the discussion between the AMHP and ambulance control should make the exact circumstances of the situation completely clear. If any difficulties arise, the AMHP should ask to be referred to the Duty Communications Officer at ambulance control, and ask for backup from a more senior AMHP/manager.

Evidencing problems

Conveyance to hospital is a significant problem in many areas of the country, and it is not uncommon to hear about incidents where an MHA assessment conveyance request is 'bumped down' the response list as more 'urgent' and life-threatening problems are referred into the service.

In order to evidence problems, and make it more likely that commissioners can be persuaded to sort out alternative conveyance arrangements where AMHPs face problems, it is important that they provide evidence of the difficulties that have occurred.

The following suggestions might be worth considering:

1 Keep a record of each occasion where transport has been delayed beyond a specified period of time (for example, two hours between the end of the assessment and the admission onto a ward).
2 Note the impact of the delay on the service user, their family and community and any increase in risks as a result.
3 Note any potential additional resources (such as extra police support, doctors needing to remain on site, etc.) and any potential costs.
4 Consider using Trust incident reporting systems to record and highlight the problems you are encountering. This will also have the effect of 'escalating' the problems you are facing to staff in senior positions within the organisations.
5 If you are being put at risk, consider involving your union or professional body.

Transporting patients over long distances

AMHPs may need to help organise conveyance and admission over a long distance in the following circumstances:

• There are no locally available beds.
• The patient requires a specialist service which is only available outside of the local area.
• The patient has come from a different area, and needs to return to that area for admission.

In such circumstances, it will be useful to consider the following:

• Conveying patients across organisational boundaries can cause particular problems. This is one reason why some patients, even though geographically close to their 'home', are admitted locally but transferred later. Any operational and resourcing issues should be negotiated between the duty ambulance control room manager, the local duty police inspector, and the appropriate AMHP or LSSA duty manager. If this can happen ahead of time it is most helpful.

- The patient (and the cost of conveyance) remains the responsibility of the area in which they *ordinarily reside*. In situations where the patient is assessed out of area, this means that the bed manager or AMHP from the area where the patient is located will need to negotiate with the bed manager or commissioner from the home area to agree on whether they would rather pay for a private bed or a private ambulance, where that choice is a practical alternative.
- Where the AMHP is the applicant in these circumstances, they still have the duty to ensure that all necessary arrangements are made for the patient to be conveyed to the hospital and will need to consult closely with NHS staff identifying the available bed.
- Ensuring that the receiving hospital has all necessary papers and information about the person being admitted is especially important. Where it is logistically possible to do so, emailing copies of the legal papers and AMHP report ahead to the receiving hospital can be very helpful. For example, if there are any minor errors on the paperwork, these can be spotted ahead of time and corrected. Additionally, some hospitals require evidence of recommendations and applications before they will locate a bed.
- Although the AMHP will still have responsibility for the safe conveyance and admission of the patient, and would normally be expected to accompany the patient to the receiving hospital, this responsibility may be delegated.
- In circumstances where an AMHP delegates their authority, it is still important to double-check that the hospital has received the patient.
- The need to transport someone some distance may mean medical staff need to consider sedating the patient prior to conveyance. Where no nurse escort is available for a patient who has been sedated, a paramedic crew with advanced life support skills should be requested in case of adverse drug reaction, cessation of breathing, etc., with the attending clinician giving clear instructions at handover on likely adverse reactions and treatment required (CoP 17.7).

Conveyance to hospital: guidance on powers

A person who is to be conveyed to any place under any provision of the Mental Health Act is deemed to be in legal custody (s137(1)). Anyone who is responsible for conveying or detaining a person under the terms of the Act has all the powers, authorities, protection and privileges of a police constable (s137(2)).

The AMHP responsible may call upon others to assist in performing functions of the Act. Anyone obstructing a person in this exercise of their duty shall be guilty of an offence and will be liable to arrest (s129(1)(d)).

Anyone who escapes while in legal custody may be retaken by the person who had legal custody of the patient immediately before the escape, or by any police constable or AMHP (s138(1)(a)).

Conveyance to hospital: papers you need to make sure you have with you

The AMHP should have available:

- a completed application form and recommendations for detention in hospital;
- appropriate identification issued by the LSSA they are acting on behalf of;
- forms recording the 'Delegation of Authority to Convey a Patient to a Hospital under the Mental Health Act';
- any recorded risk assessment and risk management plan relating to the conveyance of the patient;
- any report from doctors concerning their observations around the risks associated with the patient, and how to manage them once on the ward;
- a copy of an initial AMHP assessment report, with basic information about the patient and their social situation and reason for admission.

Checklist: conveyance

✓ A properly completed application for admission under the MHA, together with the required medical recommendations, gives the AMHP the authority to convey the patient to hospital.

✓ A patient should be conveyed to hospital in the most humane and least threatening way, consistent with ensuring that no harm comes to the patient or to others.

✓ AMHPs authorised to convey under the MHA will have all the powers of a police constable in respect of, and for the duration of, the conveyance of the patient. They may delegate the power to convey to other people, such as ambulance staff or the police. If so, it would be sensible to do so in writing.

✓ All detained patients should be conveyed to hospital by an appropriate vehicle and with suitably trained staff. In most cases this is likely to be an ambulance (but need not be, as long as the alternative is suitable and safe). In situations where the risk of injury to patients or staff is likely, the assistance of the police may be required. The use of a police van could be considered if the patient is violent.

✓ The patient should only be conveyed by private car in exceptional circumstances and if the AMHP is satisfied that the patient does not present a danger to themselves or others. There should always be at least one escort for the patient other than the driver. The car driver must have appropriate car insurance cover.

✓ Where someone is being conveyed to a place of safety under s135(1) of the Act, the organising of the conveyance arrangements will be the responsibility of the AMHP.

✓ Patients who have been sedated should always be accompanied by a health professional who can understand the patient and their needs and has access to necessary emergency equipment.

Checklist: final arrangements

✓ Call ahead and make sure the ward is expecting the patient, and confirm who will be receiving them and the legal papers.

✓ Make sure you have the address and details of the ward written down correctly on the AMHP application form.

✓ Encourage/support the patient to put together a case of clothes and necessary belongings (where appropriate).

✓ Check whether any practical arrangements need to be made for pets, to stop milk deliveries, and so on.

✓ Check the fridge and negotiate with the patient about disposing of any perishable materials.

✓ Make sure the property is secure before you leave, for example checking windows and doors are locked.

✓ Double-check there are no adults with care and support needs or children who may need additional support and make arrangements as necessary.

Implementing decisions: admission to hospital – a guide for receiving nurses

When a patient is being admitted on the application of an approved mental health professional (AMHP), the receiving officer should go through the documents and check their accuracy with the AMHP.

CoP 35.9

Checklist: for admitting nurses

Nurses on wards may be authorised in writing by hospital managers to receive applications and recommendations for detention in hospital.

✓ A properly completed application form and recommendations provides managers of the admitting hospital with the authority to detain the patient, however, even if the papers are properly completed there is no legal obligation on the hospital to accept them.

✓ Record time and date of admission on form H3.

✓ If the patient is already in hospital (for example, as an informal patient) the date of admission will still be the date the application was accepted by the hospital managers.

The nurse should check all the papers and make sure:

✓ that the names and addresses on all the forms match
✓ that all of the papers are signed and dated
✓ that the application has been signed after the recommendations
✓ that there are no more than five days between the two medical recommendations, and not more than 14 days between the last medical recommendation and the application and admission.

Minor errors can be amended by the person who signed the original form, as long as they do so within 14 days of the admission date (s15).

Remember!

A faulty emergency (s4) application may not be corrected after it has ceased to have effect (i.e. 72 hours) unless it has (in effect) become an s2 application because a second medical recommendation has been received.

An application or recommendation which is found to be incorrect or defective can be amended by the person who signed it, with the consent of the managers of the hospital, within the period of 14 days starting on the date of the patient's admission.

Checklist: correctable faults

✓ leaving blank any spaces on the form which should have been filled in (other than the signature)
✓ failure to delete one or more alternatives in places where only one can be correct
✓ minor discrepancies concerning the names on the forms
✓ discrepancies in address details between the different forms

However, some errors are so significant they cannot be amended, and make the application invalid (CoP 35.13).

Checklist: mistakes which invalidate an application

✓ The application is not accompanied by the correct number of medical recommendations.
✓ There are more than five days between the two medical recommendations.

✓ The application and the recommendations do not all relate to the same patient (i.e. have fundamentally different names on them).

✓ An application or recommendation is not signed at all, or is signed by someone not qualified to do so.

✓ The recommendations or applications do not comply with the conflict of interest regulations.

✓ Neither of the doctors were s12 approved, or the AMHP was not in reality an AMHP at the point where the application was made.

✓ An application does not specify the correct hospital (an application cannot be addressed to a Trust; it must be addressed to a specific hospital).

If this happens, a new assessment would need to be arranged. However, depending on what or where the error is, it may be possible to use one or more of the recommendations.

If admission documents reveal a defect which fundamentally invalidates the application and which cannot, therefore, be rectified under section 15 of the Act, the patient can no longer be detained on the basis of the application. Authority for the patient's detention can be obtained only through a new application (or, in the interim, by the use of the holding powers under section 5 if the patient has already been admitted to the hospital). Unless that authority is to be sought, the hospital managers should use their power under section 23 to discharge the patient. The patient should be informed both orally and in writing, and in an accessible format for the patient.

CoP 35.13

Remember!

The admission of a patient on the basis of an application for treatment s3 (but not assessment for s2) automatically causes any previous application for admission, or for guardianship, or for supervised community treatment, to cease to have effect.

Using electronic forms

It is now possible to submit recommendations and applications electronically. In addition you can download electronic copies of forms from the website. The form will not be invalidated if optional text is deleted by the author, as is possible in the electronic version of the form (such as choices between reasons for admission). However, you may wish to make clear where deletions have been made by using the strikethrough functionality.[1]

Examples from practice

Salaam's case

Salaam was an informal patient, and was assessed on the Friday for detention under s2. The doctors saw the patient separately, and the AMHP interviewed him with the second doctor.

On the Monday, the MHA administrator realised that one doctor was supervised by the other in their day-to-day work – as a result, the two doctors did not meet the conflict of interest regulations related to professional relationship. Salaam was placed on a 5(2), the AMHP was called and arranged for an independent s12 doctor to attend, and that person made a new recommendation for Salaam's detention. The AMHP then made a new application (because the application needed to post-date the recommendation).

Salaam was judged to have been 'formally' admitted on the form H3 on the Monday.

Connor's case

Connor was seen by the AMHP and doctors on 10 April and admitted under s3 on the same day. A week later (on the 17 April) the AMHP's manager contacted the MHA administrator because it had come to his attention that the AMHP's professional registration with the nursing and midwifery council had been allowed to lapse. He had ceased to be a registered nurse on 1 April.

Because of this, his approval as an AMHP had ended and he was not legally able to sign application forms after 31 March. This meant that the application form for Connor, and his subsequent detention, were illegal. Connor was informed, and placed on an s5(2). Another AMHP was instructed to undertake the assessment.

Because she was able to talk to both doctors, and was satisfied that Connor's situation and presentation remained the same, the AMHP chose to use the existing joint medical recommendation from 10 April and, after assessing Connor herself, made a new application on 18 April (within 14 days of the medical examinations).

Best practice guidance: actions following arrival on the ward

- Ensure the patient is aware of their status and of what is likely to happen next.
- Introduce the patient to the receiving nurse or coordinator and complete the handover, checking that statutory forms are correct.

- Complete the outline report and inform the NR and other appropriate persons of safe arrival and thank the police and/or ambulance services for their assistance.

Implementing decisions: the AMHP outline report

Where a patient is admitted under the MHA, in accordance with paragraph 14.93 of the CoP, the AMHP should leave an outline report, giving reasons for the admission and any practical matters of the patient's circumstances that the hospital should know (see Appendix 3 for a specimen AMHP outline report). It must contain basic information about risk and reasons for admission, as well as the name and contact details of the AMHP in case ward staff need to contact them urgently, before the main report reaches the ward.

In some areas, doctors also complete a short report to make sure ward staff are aware of essential risk information, and to provide guidance to more junior members of staff about how the patient should be managed after admission (see Appendix 3 for a sample report).

Some AMHPs might think it is sufficient to leave a verbal interim report with the nurse who accepts the section papers prior to the delivery of the outline report. However, this practice ought to be avoided. Written reports both protect the AMHP and ensure that the patient gets the care that they need.

> An outline report does not take the place of the full report which AMHPs are expected to complete for their employer (or the local authority on whose behalf they are acting – if different).
>
> CoP 14.95

Implementing decisions: patient rights, section 132

Although the Code of Practice expects an AMHP to explain a patient's rights of appeal to the patient, s132 gives a duty to the hospital managers to give patients their rights. Chapter 4 of the Code of Practice gives guidance to hospitals regarding their responsibilities in this area.

These responsibilities are invariably delegated to the ward staff and it is the ward staff who are expected to use all possible means to give the information to the patient. This is particularly important when a patient lacks capacity, has fluctuating capacity, or has other cognitive deficits or communication problems. Ward staff have a responsibility to ensure that patients continue to understand the information given to them about their rights.

Mental health provider trusts will have policies, procedures and processes of recording how and when patients are given their rights at regular intervals. Do you know what your inpatient unit's policy is?

✓

Summary checklist: forms

✓ Sections 2 and 3 require two medical recommendations (two separate or one joint). Joint recommendations should only be used if both doctors carry out the assessment together.

Section 4 requires only one medical recommendation.

✓ One doctor providing a recommendation must be qualified under s12 of the Act. The second medical recommendation should if practicable be provided by a doctor who has a prior acquaintance with the patient, or is also approved under s12.

✓ If a joint recommendation is used, please ensure that both doctors enter their full names and addresses.

✓ Are there any obvious conflicts of interest between the different assessors? For example, does one doctor work under the direction of the other?

✓ Are the patient's name and address the same on all of the documents?

✓ The patient must have been examined by both doctors within seven days of each other – i.e. with a maximum of five clear days between examinations.

✓ If neither of the doctors had previous acquaintance with the patient, ensure that the AMHP has stated the reasons why a recommendation could not be obtained from a doctor who was acquainted with the patient, on the application.

✓ Is each form signed and correctly dated?

✓ Please ensure that non-applicable statements are deleted where specified.

✓ Make sure the application names the admitting hospital, not just the trust's name.

Summary

- Completing legal papers and reports is an essential part of the assessment process.
- It is important to take time with papers, to avoid having to make changes later, or risk a patient being detained illegally.
- It is also essential to make sure ward staff have all the information they need about the risks and requirements the patient has.
- If you are regularly running into problems with access to beds, or waiting long periods for conveyance, make sure you report these problems, using health governance systems if appropriate.

Note

1 www.gov.uk/government/publications/electronic-communication-of-statutory-forms-under-the-mental-health-act

5   Working with compulsion in the community

This chapter aims to help AMHPs, responsible clinicians and other professionals understand the options available to support longer term care or treatment in the community.

By the end of the chapter, you should:

- have a clearer understanding of the different powers available under s3, community treatment orders (s17A), guardianship (s7) and the Deprivation of Liberty Safeguards (MCA)
- be able to make informed choices between the different powers
- be able to decide how best to use the powers that exist to support patients

Introduction

The introduction of the amended Act in 2008 reflected parliament's desire to update the law to make it more appropriate to the current situation, by introducing new options for supporting and protecting people with long-term mental health and mental capacity needs – both in hospital and in the community.

However, it should be remembered that the majority of people with whom we work do so on a basis of choice, not compulsion. In each case, consideration of a less restrictive alternative should always be the starting point.

Comparisons between the different powers available

A range of powers now exists to support people in need of longer-term care. An important starting point when thinking about which power might be most appropriate to a particular situation is that of understanding the ethos or underlying principles of the two Acts involved – the MHA and the MCA.

When considering whether to use powers of the MHA or MCA, the overall purpose of the intervention needed and whether a lack of capacity exists are key issues (see Table 5.1).

Table 5.1 Fitting needs to the powers available

Purpose of intervention	Likely intervention route
A person with capacity needs treatment for a mental disorder in hospital, which they are unwilling to agree to	MHA s3
A person without capacity to make the decision, needs to be treated for a mental disorder in hospital, in conditions that would amount to a deprivation of their liberty	MHA s3
The person can have leave from hospital of more than seven days (in one go or when combined), but it isn't yet clear whether the leave will be successful, or the plan is not yet in place	s17 leave
The person lacks capacity to make decisions about where they should live, is ready to leave hospital, but the care plan needed to keep themselves safe amounts to a deprivation of their liberty	Deprivation of Liberty Safeguards
The person has capacity to make decisions about where they should live, is ready to leave hospital, but the risks are such that they can only really be managed by a community care plan that deprives them of their liberty (e.g. one where they will need to be accompanied whenever they leave the placement)	S17 leave (extended)
The person needs ongoing medical treatment for a mental disorder, but can only be safely discharged from hospital if the RC has the power to recall them	Community treatment order (MHA s17A)
The care that the person needs can be provided in the community, but only within a structured care plan that places some restrictions on their liberty (such as where they should live) but does not detain them there	Guardianship (MHA s7)
You need to have the authority to take someone to where they should live, or return them if they leave (for example, where there is a risk someone will return to live on the streets)	Guardianship (MHA s7)
You need to prevent someone who lacks capacity from leaving the place that they need to be in order to receive care	Deprivation of Liberty Safeguards/ Court of Protection
You need to stop someone who has a mental disorder and lacks capacity from leaving hospital where they are receiving care or treatment for a physical condition rather than a mental disorder	Deprivation of Liberty Safeguards
The person has capacity, but is vulnerable to exploitation or abuse and needs to be supported in a way that will deprive them of their liberty	The Inherent Jurisdiction of the high court may be used to provide appropriate safeguards

In practice, decisions may not be as clear cut as Table 5.1 suggests. For example, there have been situations where a DoLS Order has been used alongside a CTO or guardianship order. However, it will provide a useful starting point from which to begin discussions concerning what, if any, compulsory powers will be needed.

We now go on to consider the powers in more detail.

S3/extended s17 leave: CoP chapter 31

Mental health system

The patient is already detained on s3.

Application process

See Chapter 3, page 90.

Process for use of extended s17 leave

- The responsible clinician must be able to justify why a CTO in particular is not a suitable alternative.
- The Code (chapter 31) provides this advice on pointers towards s17 leave as opposed to using a CTO (see Table 5.2).

Since the Supreme Court made its decisions in the MM and PJ cases (https://www.supremecourt.uk/cases/docs/uksc-2018-0037-judgment. pdf; https://www.supremecourt.uk/cases/docs/uksc-2017-0212-judgment. pdf) that neither a CTO nor conditional discharge under Part III of the Act could be used to deprive someone of their liberty in the community (even if the person had capacity and agreed), the only way to support a small number of very risky patients has been to either use extended s17 leave, a concurrent DoLS Order, or approach the High Court to request that it use its inherent jurisdiction powers to provide a legal framework.

Authorising community plans (including for forensic patients) that amount to a deprivation of liberty

Consider whether the community care plan is likely to amount to a deprivation of liberty. If it does, legal authority will be needed to authorise the plan.

Neither a CTO or guardianship can be used to authorise a community plan that results in a deprivation of liberty. The same is true for conditions agreed for conditional discharge into the community. Additionally, the person themselves (even if they have capacity) *cannot* agree to be deprived of their liberty.

Table 5.2 CTO or longer term leave of absence: relevant factors to consider (CoP 31.7)

Factors suggesting longer-term leave	Factors suggesting CTO
• Discharge from hospital is for a specific purpose or a fixed period	• There is confidence that the patient is ready for discharge from hospital on an indefinite basis
• The patient's discharge from hospital is deliberately on a 'trial' basis	• There are good reasons to expect that the patient will not need to be detained for the treatment they need to be given
• The patient is likely to need further in-patient treatment without their consent or compliance	• The patient appears prepared to consent or comply with the treatment they need – but risks as below mean that recall may be necessary
• There is a serious risk of arrangements in the community breaking down or being unsatisfactory – more so than for CTO	• The risk of arrangements in the community breaking down, or of the patient needing to be recalled to hospital for treatment, is sufficiently serious to justify CTO, but not to the extent that it is very likely to happen

Timescales and safeguards

- The s3 that underpins the s17 leave can last for up to six months (followed by periods of six months and a year), and the patient has a right of appeal in each 'period' of detention to both the hospital managers and the independent Tribunal service.
- The NR is able to request discharge (which must be in writing and allow 72-hours' notice) but this can be blocked by the responsible clinician in situations where, in their opinion, if discharged the patient would act in a way dangerous to others or to themselves (s25(1) MHA).
- On each occasion when the RC wanted to grant additional extended leave, they would need to be able to justify why a CTO was not appropriate.
- Renewal of s3 needs the written the agreement of the responsible clinician, and a second professional who is concerned with the planning, management or delivery of treatment for the patient (who must be from a different professional group from the RC, for example, an AMHP or CPN.

Treatment rules

Part 4 of the MHA applies and allows for the compulsory administration of medication. For the first three months, the clinician in charge of the treatment can authorise this, even without the consent of the patient. (The three months starts from the point the person was first given medication for mental disorder while detained, so if they were detained on s2, which was then converted to s3, the three-month period may start from the beginning of the s2.) After three months, the responsible clinician can only continue with treatment with the patient's consent, or with the agreement of an externally appointed doctor (a second opinion appointed doctor (SOAD)).

Advantages and disadvantages of using s3 to support ongoing care in the community (as extended s17 leave)

Advantages

- The patient is still covered by part 4 of the MHA, so can be required to take medication in the community.
- The RC can rescind the s17 leave at any time and return the patient to hospital. There is no requirement to involve other professionals in this decision.
- The patient has access to the support of an IMHA (but would also have this under CTO).
- Being on s17 leave allows the RC to use a care plan in the community that amounts to a deprivation of the person's liberty.

Disadvantages

- Tribunals are likely to look closely at why s17 leave is appropriate and why (for example) a CTO is not used.
- The patient has fewer rights when on s17 leave compared to being a community patient on a CTO. For example, if the CTO is revoked and the patient returns to hospital under section 3 the hospital managers must refer the case to Tribunal.
- A patient with capacity has rights to make advance decisions and appoint an LPA while in the community on a CTO, and can also refuse medication/treatment. Although these options are available to a patient on s17 leave, the patient remains subject to the powers of s3 and the MHA takes precedence (so treatment could be enforced).

S7 (guardianship): Reference Guide chapter 28; Code of Practice chapter 30

> in large part, the effectiveness of guardianship relies on the moral (rather than legal) authority of guardians and the quality of their relationship with the patient.
>
> Reference Guide 28.9
>
> Guardianship may not have teeth, but it does have very tough gums.
>
> Quote from an AMHP lead, Nov 2022

Social service system

Although this is a section of the MHA, it is a power that is the responsibility of the local social service authority (LSSA). The 'guardian' may be a private individual (approved by the LSSA) but in most cases it is the LSSA itself, and as an organisation they nominate a social worker to take on the powers.

The purpose of guardianship is to enable patients to receive care outside hospital when it cannot be provided without the use of compulsory powers. Such care may, or may not, include specialist medical treatment for mental disorder.

CoP 30.2

Guardianship therefore provides an authoritative framework for working with a patient, with a minimum of constraint, to achieve as independent a life as possible within the community. Where it is used, it should be part of the patient's overall care plan ...

CoP 30.4

The 'responsible' local authority for guardianship is the one receiving the application – in practice this is most likely to be the LSSA with 'ordinary residence' responsibility for the patient. The exception is where there is a private guardian. In this case the responsible LSSA is the one in whose area the private guardian lives.

Application process

- Applications are to the LSSA.
- Two doctors (including one s12 doctor) must recommend guardianship, and an AMHP must be satisfied that an application should be made.
- The AMHP must consult the nearest relative, and if the nearest relative objects, the guardianship cannot proceed.
- The application must be sent to the LSSA within 14 days of the second medical recommendation.
- The person receiving the papers does not need to be the director themselves; it can be any representative appointed by the LSSA.
- Additionally, courts can also make a guardianship order provided that they comply with the appropriate processes and the LSSA is willing to accept it (see Reference Guide 28.64/MHA s37).
- There is no statutory limit between the receipt of the application and its being accepted by the relevant director. However, clearly if there is a very significant delay between the application and the acceptance, its validity might be called into question.

- The guardianship application will only come into effect once it is accepted by the relevant LSSA.
- It is possible to transfer someone to guardianship under s19 of the Act (i.e. for someone already detained in hospital). If this is done, most authorities would still require evidence that the use of guardianship is necessary and appropriate (such as a report from an AMHP) together with a care plan detailing the powers that are required. Hospital managers need to sign the first section of the transfer form, and LSSAs the second section. The LSSA representative must also state the date on which the person will be transferred into guardianship on this form.

Remember!

It is important to be aware of the fact that where a person is transferred into guardianship from s3, the first guardianship period will last for what would have been the remainder of the pre-existing section (whether this is two months or ten months).

The criteria in detail

An application for guardianship may be made, in relation to a person who is aged 16 or over and who is not a ward of court, on the grounds that:

- the patient is suffering from mental disorder of a nature or degree which warrants their reception into guardianship, and
- it is necessary, in the interests of the welfare of the patient or for the protection of other persons, that the patient should be so received.

CoP 30.8

Mental disorder of a nature or degree

For the use of guardianship, mental disorder has the same wide definition as in other parts of the Act, except that the learning disability qualification applies. This means that where the only reason for using guardianship with someone with a learning disability is their learning disability, this must be associated with 'abnormally aggressive or seriously irresponsible conduct' on their behalf.

This qualification has the effect that it excludes many people with a learning disability, but includes people with a head injury or conditions such as Asperger syndrome. However, it is perfectly possible for someone with a learning disability and a mental illness to be made subject to guardianship on the basis of their mental illness. 'Nature or degree' has the same meaning as in the rest of the MHA (see p.93).

Necessary in the interests of the person's welfare or for the protection of other people: how to consider the issue of 'necessity'

It will need to be demonstrated that one of the three powers (or requirements) available with guardianship is needed, namely:

1 the power to require the patient to reside at a specific place (and/or the ability to take them to or return them to that place);
2 the power to require the patient to attend at places and times for the purpose of medical treatment, occupation, education or training (this does not include any power to enforce treatment);
3 the power to require access to the patient by an AMHP or other specified person.

Guardianship is most likely to be appropriate where:

- the patient is thought to be likely to respond well to the authority and attention of a guardian and so be more willing to comply with necessary treatment and care for their mental disorder, and
- there is a particular need for someone to have the authority to decide where the patient should live or to insist that doctors, AMHPs or other people be given access to the patient.

CoP 30.9

In practice the service user does not have to agree with the care plan, but they do need to *acknowledge* it. Which approach is adopted may depend on the nature or degree of the person's capacity to make decisions about their own care. For someone with advanced dementia, guardianship may offer a protective framework within which care can be provided. For someone with a moderate learning disability, guardianship might offer an 'authoritative' framework which makes it more likely that they will comply with the care plan.

Finally, guardianship cannot be used to 'detain' someone. How to determine what is 'detention' and what is 'restriction' is a point of professional judgement, but the key question is, do you need to stop someone leaving the place where care is provided, or is it that you need the authority to bring them back should they not return? Guardianship provides the power to return the patient to the place they are required to live, but not the power to stop them leaving in the first place.

Remember!

The Supreme Court judgement on the meaning of deprivation of liberty applies as much to guardianship as other forms of state intervention in the lives of citizens. Therefore, AMHPs will need to be satisfied that the use of guardianship will not involve 'continuous supervision and control, and not being free to leave'. If this is required, DoLS on its own may need to be considered, or DoLS plus guardianship might be an option. Alternatively, where the person has capacity to make decisions about where they should live, and the support they need (meaning DoLS is not available, even if guardianship is) an alternative legal framework, such as an application to Court, may need to be considered.

Role of the recommending doctors

Patients need to be assessed by two doctors (in a similar way to assessments for s2 or s3) and recommendations (forms G3 or G4) made prior to an AMHP making an application for guardianship.

Section 12 and the Conflict of interest regulations apply to assessments for guardianship, so at least one of the two doctors needs to be s12 approved, and if that doctor does not know the patient, if possible the second doctor should. If the patient has particular needs (for example, they have a learning disability, a personality disorder or a hearing impairment) it would be useful if one of the recommending doctors also had expertise in this area.

The doctors must see the patient not more than five days apart, and the AMHP must see the patient and sign their application within 14 days of the second medical examination for recommendation.

Role of the AMHP

As with other MHA assessments, an AMHP can be instructed by the LSSA to take the case into consideration which may lead to the setting up of and undertaking of an MHA assessment to consider whether guardianship is appropriate.

In practice, this means that the AMHP should coordinate the process, ensure that the most appropriate medical assessors are selected, and identify and consult the NR to ensure that they do not object to the use of the guardianship. If the NR does object, the application cannot go forward unless a successful case for displacement is made to the courts (see pp.74–80) The AMHP must also satisfy themselves that the patient is over 16 years of age and not a ward of court.

AMHPs also need to be satisfied that the guardianship criteria are met, but in addition it is important that AMHPs are satisfied – 'having regard to any wishes expressed by relatives of the patient or any other relevant circumstances' (s13 1A(b)) – that an application should be made. Therefore, considering the wider social and cultural situation of the patient, including the impact of the use of guardianship, is an important aspect of the decision-making process.

> An application for guardianship should be accompanied by a comprehensive care plan established on the basis of multi-disciplinary discussions in accordance with the care programme approach (or its equivalent).
>
> CoP 30.20

Care planning

It is important that the person on guardianship and others are as clear about the requirements of an order as possible. If during the life of the order you wish to change the requirements, it would be good practice to let all those involved, including the patient, know this in writing.

Timescales and safeguards

- Guardianship lasts for two periods of six months and then periods of 12 months. The initial period of six months will differ if the patient has been transferred under s19 of the Act into guardianship. The guardianship will in that case be regarded as starting on the date of the original detention.
- The same timescales that apply to applications for admission also apply to guardianship. So there must be no more than five days between medical recommendations being made, and the application must be signed within 14 days of seeing and assessing the person. Finally, the guardianship application must be received by the local authority within 14 days of the second medical recommendation.
- The NR can object to the use of the order, and this objection can only be overturned by the county court if the conditions for displacement under s29 MHA are met.
- The patient has a right of appeal during each period of detention. The appeals can be made to both to the MHRT service and/or the LSSA.
- Someone on guardianship has the right of access to an IMHA.
- The LSSA has an obligation to provide information (orally and in writing) to the patient on guardianship and (as long as the patient doesn't object) to the NR about the patient's rights and the ability of the NR to discharge the order.

- The NR also has an absolute right of discharge. Unlike for s3, this cannot be blocked by the LSSA (although the option of applying for displacement, and making a new application for guardianship would still be available).

See the Reference Guide, chapter 28 for more details about guardianship processes.

Process for renewal

- In the two months before the order is due to expire, the patient needs to be examined by their 'appropriate practitioner'. In most cases this will be an approved clinician appointed by the LSSA to complete this task. In the case of someone with a private guardian, this would be their 'nominated medical attendant'. If that person is satisfied that the person still meets the criteria, they need to provide a report to that effect to the LSSA. In addition to this report, the doctor must also complete a recommendation form (G9) to recommend renewal of the guardianship order.
- In addition, it would be good practice for an AMHP or the person's care coordinator to provide a copy of the current care plan, and an explanation of why the use of the order is still appropriate.
- Finally, it is expected that the LSSA will always consider whether or not to discharge the guardianship order at the point of renewal.
- If renewal is agreed, the new period of compulsion will start on the date when the current guardianship is due to expire (rather than the date of the AC's report, or the LSSA's decision).

What to do if the patient leaves the place they are expected to live

If there is a requirement on the patient to live in a particular place, and they ignore that requirement and leave, they become formally 'absent without leave' (AWOL).
A patient who is AWOL in this way may be taken into custody under s18(3) by:

- any officer on the staff of any local authority;
- any police officer, or other constable; or
- any person authorised in writing by the patient's guardian or any local authority.

Time limits for return:

- six months from the point the person went AWOL or
- the date the guardianship was due to expire (whichever is longer).

Ending of guardianship

Guardianship can be discharged/ended by:

- the nearest relative (except where the guardianship was started by the courts);

- the responsible clinician;
- the LSSA or their Appeals Committee;
- the patient being admitted under s3 of the MHA (but not s2 or s4);
- the patient being in prison for more than six months;
- a decision of the Mental Health Act Tribunal.

If you come to the conclusion that guardianship is no longer appropriate, you should bring your concerns to the attention of the LSSA, together with any alternative views that may be expressed by other professionals or the person's NR.

Transfer back to hospital for treatment

If transfer back to hospital under s3 is being considered, two doctors and an AMHP must see the patient and make appropriate recommendations and an application for s3. If the patient is transferred back to hospital on s3 in this manner, their detention will last as long as the guardianship was due to last.

Remember!

Neither a private guardian nor a nominated medical officer can discharge a guardianship order. Of course, if the private guardian is also the NR, they could discharge on that basis.

MCA interface issues and treatment rules

- A deputy from the Court of Protection, and someone who has a welfare LPA, cannot oppose a requirement imposed by a guardian (such as where a person should live). However, if the LPA recipient is also the NR, they may discharge the person from the guardianship order.
- The guardianship order *provides no authority to enforce treatment on a person*. Treatment can be provided:
  ○ with the person's valid consent;
  ○ when agreed by a Deputy or someone with a relevant LPA (see p.17);
  ○ or if the person lacks capacity, in their best interests.
- Guardianship *does not authorise a deprivation of liberty*, i.e. you can take someone to the place you want them to be, and bring them back if they leave and refuse to return, but you cannot detain them if they wish to go out into the community. You can however use a DoLS order alongside guardianship if the person lacks capacity.

Advantages and disadvantages of guardianship orders

Advantages

- The focus is on the person's welfare, not on medical treatment.
- It provides an authoritative framework within which to work with individuals who need it in order to remain in the community.
- The need to go to court in a situation where the NR objects provides a balance against the arbitrary use of the powers – in contrast to the use of DoLS, where the only option for a relative who is unhappy with a decision to use a DoLS order is an appeal to the Court of Protection. (However, case law has made it clear that the objection or disagreement of friends or relatives to a DoLS order should indicate the need to take a case to the Court of Protection to decide whether the placement and the deprivation is in the person's best interests.)
- Guardianship can provide the authority to tell someone where they must live in the community, take them there, and return them if they leave; unlike a CTO, where although a condition to live in a particular place can be set, non-compliance does not provide any authority to return the patient to that place. The only option open to the RC in such circumstances would be to consider whether recall to hospital for treatment was justified.
- If used to improve compliance with a care plan, the person does not have to agree, but there does usually need to be a level of acceptance or understanding of what is required.
- Guardianship can be used in either a *residential placement or a private residence*, i.e. somewhere not registered under part 2 of the Care Standards Act 2000. (DoLS can only be used in hospital or residential care placements – community placements outside of these arrangements that resulted in a deprivation of liberty by would need to be authorised by the Court of Protection.) It cannot be used in hospital (except for a very short time while a placement is being organised).

Disadvantages

- Guardianship does not authorise a deprivation of a person's liberty. A standard or urgent DoLS authorisation would be needed for this to occur, or an order from the courts must be obtained. These can run concurrently with the guardianship order.
- The NR can object and prevent the use of the guardianship order, and has a right of absolute discharge, which cannot be barred.
- Section 117 does not automatically apply (unless the service user has previously been detained on an s3 or its forensic equivalent) so the patient may be liable to pay for the placement they are required to live in.

> ### Remember!
>
> Although sometimes the seemingly most unlikely people do comply with guardianship orders, continual disregard for the requirements is likely to be an indication that the authority is inappropriate, and thought should be given to its discharge.

Ultimately, the successful use of guardianship will depend on the quality of the relationship between the person and their guardian. The order works by providing a 'legal scaffolding' around which that relationship can develop.

Community treatment orders s17a Code of Practice chapter 29; Reference Guide chapter 26

> The purpose of a CTO is to allow suitable patients to be safely treated in the community rather than under detention in hospital, and to provide a way to help prevent relapse and any harm – to the patient or to others – that this might cause. It is intended to help patients to maintain stable mental health outside hospital and to promote recovery.
>
> CoP 29.5

Health system

The lead for the use of the section is the person's RC. The emphasis is on treatment: the criteria clearly focus the use of this section on those people who are likely to have established diagnoses where a treatment is available, but where the patient themselves stops or is likely to stop taking treatment on discharge, with a resulting decline in their mental state and risk to themselves or others.

> ### Remember!
>
> The key issue RCs and AMHPs are asked to address when considering a CTO is *why in a particular case you feel you can only safely discharge someone from hospital if you have the ability to recall them to hospital if this becomes necessary.*

Application process

Only people already detained on s3 (or similar treatment-orientated unrestricted forensic sections) can be considered for a CTO. Section 17 (2A) requires that where longer term leave is being considered (defined as more than seven days taken together or separately), the RC must consider whether it is more appropriate to use a CTO (17A).

Unlike s2 or s3, applications are not, in fact, made to the hospital managers. The RC makes the CTO (in agreement with the AMHP) and furnishes the hospital managers with the original copy of the order (the CTO1). If the AMHP does not agree that a CTO should be made, or does not agree with the conditions, the CTO or conditions cannot go ahead.

The RC's and AMHPs role in the process

The RC must use form CTO1 when making the CTO.

Criteria

The RC must state that they believe the following criteria are met, and an AMHP must agree with this judgement.

> * The patient is suffering from a mental disorder of a nature or degree which makes it appropriate for the patient to receive medical treatment;
> * It is *necessary* for his or her health or safety or for the protection of other persons that the patient should receive such treatment;
> * *Subject to the patient being liable to recall . . . such treatment can be provided without his/her continuing to be detained in hospital*;
> * It is *necessary that the RC should be able to exercise the power . . .* to recall the patient to hospital;
> * Appropriate treatment is available.
>
> MHA, S17 A(5), emphasis added

What 'necessary' means in this context (s17A (6))

When weighing up how necessary the ability to recall is, the RC and AMHP need to consider the risks that might be associated with the patient were they not on a CTO, and not able to recall them, i.e. they need to consider the risk of a decline in the patient's mental health, and the risks they may pose to themselves or others as a result.

> A risk that the patient's condition will deteriorate is a significant consideration, but does not necessarily mean that the patient should be discharged onto a CTO rather than discharged. *The responsible clinician must be satisfied that the risk of harm arising from the patient's disorder is sufficiently serious to justify having the power to recall the patient to*

hospital for treatment. CTOs should only be used when there is reasonable evidence to suggest that there will be benefits to the individual. Such evidence may include:

- a clear link between non concordance with medication and relapse sufficient to have a significant impact on wellbeing requiring treatment in hospital
- clear evidence that there is a positive response to medication without an undue burden of side effects
- evidence that the CTO will promote recovery, and
- evidence that recall may be necessary (rather than informal admission or reassessment under the Act).

(CoP 29.16, emphasis added)

There are no conditions related to age. Therefore a young person under the age of 18 can go onto this order. There are some special considerations for child CTO patients (see CoP chapter 19).

Setting conditions

The CTO *must* include the following conditions:

- that the patient must make himself or herself available for medical examination as to whether their CTO should be extended under s20A;
- that if a SOAD doctor needs to see them, they must also make themselves available for medical examination.

The RC *may* include other conditions (subject to the agreement of the AMHP) as long as any condition is *necessary or appropriate* for one or more of the following purposes:

- ensuring the patient receives medical treatment for mental disorder; or
- preventing the risk of harm to the patient's health or safety; or
- protecting other people.

If conditions do not meet the above criteria, they cannot be made.

The RC can vary or suspend any of the conditions imposed after the order has started, without the agreement of the AMHP. However, changing recently agreed conditions without evidence of a change in circumstances is likely to be seen as poor practice. The RC doesn't need to complete a form when suspending conditions (although clearly it would be sensible to record the reasons), but when varying conditions they should use form CT02.

The AMHP's role in the process

> … The AMHP should meet with the patient before deciding whether to agree that the CTO should be made …
>
> CoP 29.22

The AMHP must sign a supporting statement on form CT01 saying they agree the criteria are met and also that is it *appropriate* to make the order. The AMHP also has to agree that any conditions imposed are necessary or appropriate.

Necessary or appropriate

As with guardianship, the requirements that an AMHP must decide whether the use of an order is 'appropriate' and whether the imposition of additional conditions is 'necessary or appropriate' means that an AMHP must consider the patient's wider context – their social situation. The AMHP must be convinced that in this patient's particular situation the powers are necessary or appropriate. In other words, even if the legal criteria are met, the AMHP need not agree to the making of the CTO if they are not convinced that is 'appropriate'.

> … In making that decision, the AMHP should consider the wider social context for the patient. Relevant factors may include any support networks the patient may have, the potential impact on the rest of the patient's family, and their need for support in providing care, and employment issues.
>
> CoP 29.22

Which AMHP?

The Code (29.5) makes it clear that while the ultimate responsibility for providing an AMHP to consider a CTO rests with the authority who has 'ordinary residence' responsibility for a patient, any willing AMHP can consider the case. This could for example be the AMHP already involved with the patient's care.

Conflict of interest regulations do not apply to the making of CTOs, however, the Code also says that the assessing team should be aware of potential conflicts and avoid being involved if they feel compromised (CoP 39.16).

As with an MHA assessment, it is appropriate that all AMHPs assessing someone for a CTO should complete a report explaining in more detail why they believe that the criteria are met, and why they believe that 'in all the circumstances of the case' it is appropriate for the person to be on a CTO order. This report should be kept with the notes (CoP 29.25).

A report should also be written when an order is extended, with a particular emphasis being placed on why the order is still appropriate, and why the patient could not be discharged.

If the AMHP decides that the CTO is not appropriate, it would not be appropriate for the RC to approach a different AMHP (CoP 29.25).

Understanding the effect of a CTO

The effect is to suspend the following elements of section 3:

- the requirement to *take medication* under Part IV of the Act;
- the liability to be *detained in hospital*.

The patient has to follow treatment rules found in Part IVA of the Act. The effect is that a patient who has capacity has to consent to treatment in the community, and a patient without capacity can only be treated as long as they do not object, and the treatment is in their best interests.

When a patient is recalled, their liability to take medication and be detained in hospital comes back into effect. (See processes for recall and revocation, pp. 150–54.)

Length of CTO order

The CTO lasts for six months from the point it is made, then a second period of six months, followed by recurrent periods of one year (if appropriate). If the order is revoked, the patient returns to the section they were on prior to being discharged onto the CTO. In this case, a new period of detention starts from the beginning – i.e. with a six-month period – however long the patient has been on the CTO.

Treatment in the community

People on a CTO are subject to the treatment rules contained in Part IVA of the Act as follows:

Patients with capacity

The rules mean that if the person has capacity they must consent to taking treatment or medication while they are in the community. In other words, a person with capacity would need to be recalled to hospital in order to be forced to receive treatment.

Patients without capacity in the community

Where the patient lacks capacity to consent, they may continue to be given treatment under the direction of an AC, as long as force does not need to be used because they object to the treatment. In other words as long as a patient without capacity passively accepts the treatment they need – such as a depot – that's fine. But if they start to object in some way, treatment should stop and the RC would need to consider whether the use of recall was justified. However, if there is an attorney (LPA) or deputy, or Court of Protection ruling that objects to the treatment being considered, the treatment would need to stop (CoP 24.19).

MCA interface issues

Although capacity (or the lack of it) is not a criterion for the use of a CTO, and the MCA cannot be used to justify giving CTO patients medical treatment for mental disorder, it is important to understand that some specific MCA-style protections do apply to medical treatment for someone on a CTO. A community patient who has capacity can make valid advance decisions to refuse treatment and appoint someone to hold LPA to make decisions should they lose capacity in the future.

> ## Remember!
>
> Because the patient on a CTO remains on a section of the Mental Health Act, parents cannot provide authority for treatment for children and young people.

Protections

- The patient has access to an IMHA.
- They have the right to apply both to the MHRT or the hospital managers for discharge of their order.
- The NR can request the patient's discharge (provided they were on s3 prior to being on a CTO. The NR of a CTO patient who had previously been held under criminal rather than civil sections of the Act cannot ask for discharge).
- The SOAD rules also provide protections.
- A person who is on a CTO must also be discharged from that order by the RC as soon as they no longer meet the criteria.
- An AMHP must agree that the use (or extension) of CTO not only meets the criteria, but is also is 'appropriate'.
- An AMHP must agree with any conditions that the RC wishes to impose in addition to the compulsory (and can also refuse to agree to conditions).

Process for extending an order

> ## Remember!
>
> It is important that all AMHPs complete a report explaining why they believe the patient still meets the criteria for the use of the section. It is also important

to remember that including an AMHP in the renewal process is intended as an additional protection – to stop people remaining on a CTO unnecessarily.

The extension of s17A, like guardianship, can be considered at any time in the two months prior to the ending of the order. The conditions for extension require that the RC state that the original criteria are still met. The AMHP must also state in writing (on form CTO7) that they agree the criteria are met and that it is appropriate to extend the period of the CTO.

In addition to the AMHP, the RC must also consult one or more people who have been professionally involved with the patient's medical treatment prior to extending the order.

AWOL

A CTO patient might be AWOL in two situations:

1 It is a condition of their CTO that they live in a particular place, and they have left that place.
2 They have been recalled to hospital, but have failed to return.

As with other discretionary conditions set under a CTO, not complying with a condition to live in a particular place does not on its own justify recall. However, the RC may choose to consider whether the fact that the person is not complying is evidence that their mental state is deteriorating, and they need treatment which they are objecting to, in which case they may meet the conditions for recall. Additionally, recall can only be to a hospital – not to the place where you want the person to live.

If the person has failed to comply with a recall notice, they are 'officially' AWOL, and can be taken into custody and conveyed back to the hospital.

If the patient goes AWOL close to the time that their CTO is due to be extended (so the RC is unable to see them and make a decision in this respect) the order will be extended and once returned the RC has seven days in which to decide whether to extend the order. (See Reference Guide 26.67-71 for more details.)

Recall and revocation

These are two separate processes.

- *Recall* means the patient must come back to a hospital or other place for medical treatment, for up to 72 hours. The RC for a patient can make this decision on their own.
- *Revocation* means the patient has to stay in hospital, and their legal status has been changed back to either s3 or the section to which they were subject before they left hospital to go onto a CTO (e.g. s37). The RC must have the agreement of an AMHP before someone's CTO can be revoked.

Recall: the details

The responsible clinician on their own can recall someone on a CTO to hospital. Hospital in this context can mean a clinic within the hospital grounds. The effect is that the person has to return to hospital, and can be detained and treated for up to 72 hours. However, medical treatment can only be given as long as the appropriate authority exists (e.g. the patient has been recalled within the first month of the order, or the CTO11 form has been completed so that treatment can begin immediately after the patient arrives at the hospital).

The conditions that need to be fulfilled prior to recall are that:

- the patient needs to receive treatment for mental disorder in hospital; and
- there would be a risk of harm to the health or safety of the patient or to other persons if the patient were not recalled.

If the patient does not comply with the compulsory conditions of the order (to be available to consider extending the order or to see a SOAD), they may also be recalled, but the non-compliance of other conditions *on their own* does not justify recall. In such a case, the conditions above would also need to be fulfilled.

Process for recall

The Reference Guide (26.34) says that the power to recall will become active once:

- either the patient receives the recall notice in person;
- or the notice of recall was delivered (either by hand, to the patient's address or by post) to the last known address of the patient.

When does the recall order take effect?

- If the patient is handed the notice for recall, it is effective immediately.
- If the notice is posted through the letter box, it will take effect the following day.
- If the notice is sent by first class post, it will deem to have effect two working days after it was posted.

If the patient does not agree to return to hospital of their own free will, the patient can be treated as 'absent without leave' and police support can be engaged to find and return them to the designated hospital. However, the team who know the patient should themselves make efforts to contact and persuade the person to return. The use of s135(2) may be appropriate if the patient is unwilling to allow you access to where they are living.

What to do if a CTO patient turns up unannounced

If they have already been recalled. Once they have received the recall notice, it isn't unknown for the patient to decide to present themselves at A&E or the hospital to which they have been recalled (the name of which must be on the recall papers) so make sure records clearly show that they have been recalled – and let your out-of-hours team know what is happening. Once the person presents, if the recall notice has been issued, they can be taken to the hospital base identified in the recall notice. If a bed is not available at that hospital base, you can't simply take the person to a different hospital. However, there would be nothing to stop you taking the patient to the named hospital base and then transferring them (Reference Guide 26.46–26.55). The 72 hours will be the same, however, and remember the patient's RC will need to have access to them, to decide whether to request revocation as opposed to seeing the patient, treating them and allowing them to return to their home in the community.

Alternatively, the patient may be picked up on an s136, in which case because the recall notice has already been issued, the patient can be taken to the hospital to which they have been recalled.

If they present but haven't been recalled. If a CTO patient is brought in on an s136, because it is possible to transfer between places of safety, they can be taken to a ward (or any other appropriate place willing to receive them) so that they can be seen by their own RC who can decide whether or not to recall them.

Alternatively, those assessing the patient should consider whether the grounds for recall are met, and if they are, contact the patient's RC – or out of hours, the duty RC.

If a CTO patient presents (for example at A&E) but isn't on an s136, the usual processes should be followed. Being on a CTO does not mean that informal admission cannot be considered. However, as an informally admitted CTO patient cannot be detained on an s5(2), if there is a risk they will stop complying (for example, due to the changeability of the patient's presentation and/or a past history of changing their mind after voluntary admission) it is likely that the conditions for recall may be met, and this should be considered.

When do the 72 hours start?

The liability to accept treatment does not come into effect until the patient returns to hospital. The 72 hours start from the time they get to the hospital.

When recalled, the patient must return to the hospital stated on the recall notice. (This doesn't have to be the patient's 'responsible' hospital whose managers hold the order.) However, the patient can be treated as an out-patient; they don't have to be admitted in order to administer the treatment. The exact arrangements will clearly depend on the situation and needs of the individual patient.

When a patient is recalled, the RC *must* send a copy of the recall notice to the managers of the responsible hospital.

> ## Remember!
>
> If you are involved in a patient's recall, make sure a clear decision has been made within 72 hours about what should happen next. Even if the patient comes back to hospital after being recalled under their own steam, it should not be assumed they are agreeing to stay informally. A proper assessment should be undertaken – and recorded – confirming the legal basis on which the person is remaining in hospital.

Revocation: the details

If the RC wishes to detain the person in hospital beyond the 72-hour period, they need the agreement of an AMHP. The AMHP must agree that:

- the conditions for detaining someone under s3 are met; and
- it is appropriate (having regard to all of the circumstances) to revoke the order.

If the order is revoked, the person would become subject to s3 again (or whichever section they were on prior to starting on CTO).

'Appropriate' has the same meaning here as when an application is made – i.e. the AMHP must consider the patient's situation 'in the round', interview the patient and view the requested revocation of the order in the social context of the patient. It is only after considering all the aspects of the case that revocation should be agreed. The AMHP should make a record of why they do or do not agree with the request to revoke the order.

If the RC does not ask to revoke the order, or if the AMHP does not agree the order should be revoked, the patient will be free to return to the community (at the latest, after 72 hours). It is the hospital managers' responsibility to make sure this happens.

Pros and cons of using a CTO

Pros

- The order provides a flexible way of allowing patients to leave hospital earlier than might otherwise have been the case.
- Recall can be agreed by just one person (the RC).
- There are no lower age limits, so a 15-year-old with anorexia could be discharged on a CTO, whereas neither guardianship nor DoLS would be available.
- The patient has significantly more protections than would be available were they discharged on s17 leave.
- The patient has access to an IMHA to ensure they understand their rights and can make use of them.

- At every renewal/extension of a CTO, the RC must have the agreement of an AMHP to the continuation of the order.
- During the 72-hour recall period, a CTO patient must be seen by an AMHP if the RC wants to consider revocation of CTO and reinstatement of s3. The AMHP must agree to the revocation, and can block it.

Cons

- The order continues to rely on 'moral' authority (and the patient's desire not to be readmitted) in order for it to work. If the patient continually ignores all conditions and refuses to take medication, whether or not the CTO is appropriate should be reconsidered.
- You cannot recall the patient to the place you want them to live, even if this is a condition of the order. You can only recall them to hospital. If there is a significant need to be able to return the person to a particular place, it might be useful to consider whether guardianship would be more appropriate.
- There are concerns about whether the use of CTOs actually works – you will find as many people opposed to their use, as those in favour. Indeed, the independent Wesley Report on Mental Health Law reform has recommended restricting their use, and suggested in most cases they should last no longer than 2 years.

Deprivation of liberty safeguards

Social service system

The local authority manages all referrals for a DoLS authorisation including those from health settings. However, it should also be part of the system of hospitals and care homes, as if they feel they need to care for someone who lacks capacity in a way which would amount to a deprivation of their liberty, then that organisation needs to make an application to the relevant local authority/ supervisory body for an authorisation under the DoLS processes.

Application process

Hospitals and care homes approved under the Care Act can either

- apply for a standard authorisation ahead of time (for someone they have accessed lacks capacity and would be deprived of their liberty once at the care home/ hospital) or;
- apply for an urgent authorisation (but also apply for a standard authorisation at the same time).

The original presumption was that good care management would identify ahead of time those who were likely to be deprived of their liberty, and standard applications made in advance. However, the reality has been a reliance on urgent authorisations issued by organisations once people are in placement. This fact, together with the large numbers of authorisations needed in some areas, has brought the system into disrepute, and led to calls for legal changes. The Liberty Protection Safeguards (LPS) were developed and agreed by parliament, but have yet to come into effect.

Assessment process

Once the supervisory body receives a request and decides to proceed, they need to appoint the assessors.

- There must be a minimum of two assessors (a doctor and a best interest assessor (BIA)).
- There are six areas of assessment:
  - age assessment – the person is aged over 18;
  - no objections – from a deputy at the Court of Protection or someone with an LPA;
  - has a mental disorder (this must be completed by the doctor);
  - lacks capacity to decide about whether to stay in the care home or hospital;
  - is not eligible to be admitted under the MHA (must be done by an s12 doctor or a BIA who is an AMHP);
  - it is in their best interest to be deprived of their liberty in the care home or hospital (this assessment must be complete by a trained BIA).

In reality, the doctor is often contracted to do more than one assessment (the mental capacity assessment and an eligibility assessment are most common) and the BIA is expected to at least confirm the age and that there are no objections like advance decisions to receive treatment or a decision of someone with an LPA that conflicts with something relevant to the care plan.

The BIA must also be independent of the decision-making or care management processes that resulted in the person's current situation, and must have relevant training in the DoLS processes. The doctor must also have relevant training, but may know and be treating the patient.

Example from practice: no refusals

Elle was asked as a BIA to consider the case of Albert. He had terminal cancer, and was currently in hospital awaiting treatment. His wife wanted him discharged to a hospice, but doctors on the medical ward felt that there was still beneficial treatment available to him. When Elle met with Albert's wife, she produced a signed and witnessed advance decision to refuse medical treatment, in the circumstance where he had lost capacity and treatment had a less than 50 per cent chance of success. Given that this advance decision was valid and relevant to the current situation, and treatment could therefore not be provided even if the DoL safeguard was recommended, Elle concluded that the 'no refusals' test had been failed, and the DoLS could not proceed. Elle informed the supervisory body of her decision.

Mental Capacity Act 2005, Deprivation of Liberty statistics 2022–23

300,765 applications for DoLS were received in 2022–23

(Since 2014 the numbers of requests has increased annually by between 11 and 14%)

Only 19% of applications were completed within 21 days, and the average time taken to complete applications was 153 days.

NHS digital

Timescales and safeguards

- An urgent authorisation lasts for seven days but can be extended to 14 days.
- A standard authorisation request should be completed within 28 days of being received (however, as the statistics above demonstrate, this is rarely the case).
- One of the tasks of the BIA is to recommend how long a DoLS should last – the maximum time is 12 months, but a BIA can suggest a short maximum time if they feel a situation may change.

Someone on a DoLS order can have access to an advocate, and must have a representative (if possible, someone they choose) and a right of appeal to The Court of Protection.

Legal criteria

The legal criteria 'mirror' the six assessments:

- The person must be aged 18 or over.
- There must be no relevant legal objections (i.e. LPA, advance decisions, deputies).
- They must have a mental disorder – which in this case has the same meaning as in the Mental Health Act *except* that the learning disability qualification isn't ever used.
- They must lack capacity in relation to deciding whether to stay in a particular place to receive care or treatment. Even where it is the doctor who

completes the capacity assessment, the BIA must also be satisfied that the person does lack capacity when they complete their assessment.

- It must be in their best interests to be subject to a DoLS, and the deprivation must be necessary and proportionate to the risks involved were the person not detained.

Treatment/care rules

The DoLS only authorises the deprivation of someone's liberty. Any treatment or care provided must be given with the person's consent (if they have capacity) or if they lack capacity, must be justifiable in their best interests.

> ## Remember!
>
> Even if someone lacks capacity to make particular decisions, they should still be included in the decision-making process, and their views taken into account.

Advantages and disadvantages

Advantages

- Some people may perceive it as less stigmatising, as it isn't part of the mental health legislation.
- The BIA can recommend the maximum length of the order, and can make recommendations (within limits).
- The person does have an appointed representative, and can have access to advocacy.
- It is possible to have both a DoLS and guardianship *or* a DoLS and CTO. For example, in a situation where you need to be able to stop someone leaving and bring them back (even if they resist) if they do manage to leave, a guardianship and a DoLS authorisation may be appropriate.
- Knowing that decisions about care plans could be subject to independent BIA review may be pushing up standards of decision-making and care.
- There is oversight by the Care Quality Commission (CQC).

Disadvantages

- If the representative is uninterested, or supports the placement, the person may find it difficult to access support or appeal against what is happening.
- It is a bureaucratic process, and relies on care homes and hospitals understanding when they might be depriving someone of their liberty, and making an application.

- Huge delays due to lack of resources may rob people of the rights DoLS was designed to protect.
- A professional can't 'decide' for themselves that a DoLS is needed, and make an application – the BIA must be appointed by the supervisory body, and be independent of the case.
- The only external point of appeal is The Court of Protection, where there can be delays.

'Community DoLS'

Where a person is being deprived of their liberty in a place not regulated by the CQC (supported housing placements, small group homes, a person's own home) legal authority is still needed, but will need to be obtained (at least at present) from the Court of Protection or (if they have capacity) from the High Court under its inherent jurisdiction.

Situations where DoLS might be more appropriate to someone with a mental disorder than using the Mental Health Act

This is where:

- the person has a diagnosis of a serious mental disorder (say, schizophrenia) but needs treatment for a physical health problem in circumstances where they are being deprived of their liberty;
- someone with a mental disorder lacks capacity and needs to be cared for in a community placement, and due to the risks there needs to be the authority in place to prevent them from leaving;
- they are on a psychiatric ward in circumstance where no further assessment or treatment is needed (or where the person is not objecting to taking treatment) but cannot safely be discharged until an appropriate placement becomes available.

Summary

- The aspiration of the 1983 Mental Heath Act, that the majority of people experiencing mental health problems would be able to receive help and support at home, has been largely realised.
- However, to do so, new or enhanced powers have needed to be developed to support patients and protect them and others.
- AMHPs have a particular role in ensuring that community powers are only used where it is necessary and appropriate to do so, and that their use ceases when they are no longer needed.
- All professionals have a responsibility to understand what the different options allow them to do, or not do, and to act accordingly.

Appendix 1 Local contacts for specialist groups of patient

Older people's services

┌───┐
│   │
│   │
│   │
│   │
│   │
│   │
└───┘

Mothers and babies

┌───┐
│   │
│   │
│   │
│   │
│   │
│   │
└───┘

People with eating disorders

┌───┐
│   │
│   │
│   │
│   │
│   │
│   │
└───┘

People with learning disabilities

People with personality disorders

Young people aged under 18 years

Appendix 2 Admission to hospital: hospital managers' section papers checklist

Patient's name:
Section:
Hospital number:
Previously on section:
Date of admission to hospital:
Date of implementation:
Date due to expire:
Consent due date:

Checklist:

01) Is the patient's name consistent on all papers?
02) Is the patient's address consistent on all papers?

Medical recommendations:

03) Have the two recommendations been made separately? If yes, was the patient examined by both doctors within five clear days of each other?
04) Has the patient been admitted on the section within 14 days of the last medical examination?
05) Is one practitioner approved under section 12 of the Act?
06) Are there any conflicts of interest between assessors?
07) Are the recommendations dated on or before the application?
08) Do both medical recommendations state why detention in hospital is necessary?
09) Have all relevant statements been deleted or completed as necessary?
10) Have both medical recommendations been signed and dated?

Application:

11) Has the applicant stated the capacity in which he or she is applying?
12) Has the applicant seen the patient within 14 days ending with the date of the application?

13) Is the application made and dated within 14 days of the later medical recommendation?

14) Have all the relevant statements been deleted or completed as necessary?

15) Is the application signed and dated?

16) Was the patient admitted and were the documents received within 14 days of the later of the two medical recommendations?

17) On the application, is the name and address of the hospital correct?

18) Has the patient been informed of their rights and has this been documented?

19) Have you asked if the patient wants their nearest relative informed of admission onto section?

20) Has the patient's nearest relative been informed of admission onto section?

21) Has the LSSA been named and informed of admission onto section?

22) If the application has been signed by the nearest relative, has an AMHP report been requested?

Errors that cannot be corrected:
If no to 7, 10, 15, or yes to 6, the section is invalid and we have no authority to detain. Contact the appropriate medical officer to attend and examine the patient to determine whether recommendations and an application are required.

Errors that may be corrected:
If no to 1, 2, 9 and 14, the Mental Health Act Administrator must make arrangements for the documents to be amended by the signee. The duly amended documents must be returned to the Mental Health Act Office within 14 days of the signing of the application.

Scrutinised by _____ on _____

Medical scrutiny by _____ on _____

Appendix 3   Sample reports, AMHP and Doctor

AMHP Report outline

Patient details
Patient's name, address, date of birth, age, GP, responsible clinician, care
    coordinator, patient's spoken language:
Patient's ethnicity:
Name of person appearing to be the nearest relative:
Process of identification of the nearest relative:
Nearest relative consulted or notified of application? Y/N
Information on patient's rights given? Y/N
Recording of reasons if nearest relative not notified or consulted:
Record location of assessment – community hospital ward/police station/
    A&E/s136 suite
Legal status of patient – s135, s136, under arrest, informal, s2, s5/2

Referral details
AMHP details:
Care coordinator details:
General practitioner details:
Consultant psychiatrist details:
Medical recommendation details:
Reason for request to access:
Assessment details:

AMHP assessment details
Family composition:
Reason for referral:
Social and mental health history:
Record of interview with the patient:
Record of discussions with relevant other non-professionals:
Record of discussion(s) with recommending doctor(s):
Record of discussions with other professionals:
Reasons for decision to make the application:
Alternatives to detention considered (including use of the Mental Capacity Act
    or informal admission):

Decision-making and implementation
Comments on risk to the patient, other people or to the patient's health:
Comments on capacity of the patient:

Comments on any avoidable delays in the assessment and administration
    process:
Information relating to the possibility of children visiting:
Other practical matters that the hospital should be aware of:
Property secure? Y/N/not applicable
Pets and animals accommodated? Y/N/not applicable

Name and telephone number of Local Authority contact person:

Sample reports – Doctor
This should be completed by the s12 doctor if possible: it provides the assessing
doctors with a way of passing on essential information to wards (especially if
the patient is being admitted to an out-of-area hospital) and should be attached
to other admission documents.

Date of assessment	
Name of patient	Date of birth
Address	
Brief description of relevant history:	
Brief description of mental state:	
Management, medication and risk issues:	
Name	Date

Appendix 4   The rights of the nearest relative

Taken from the Reference Guide chapter 2, Figure 5.

- The nearest relative can require the Local Authority (verbally or in writing), in which the 'patient' is living, to arrange for an approved mental health professional (AMHP) to 'consider the patient's case' including whether there is a need for compulsory admission to hospital. The local authority must inform the nearest relative in writing, of the reasons if no application for admission is made (section 13(4), Code 14.36 and 14.102).
- The nearest relative can make an application (section 11(1)), provided there are valid medical recommendation(s), for the person's compulsory admission to hospital either for assessment (section 2 – form A1) or for treatment (section 3 – form A5) or in an emergency (section 4 – form A9). The nearest relative, if the applicant, must have seen the 'patient' within 14 days (24 hours if section 4) before making an application (section 11(5)). The Code of Practice (paragraph 14.30) notes that AMHPs are 'usually a more appropriate applicant'.
- 'If the nearest relative is the applicant, any AMHP, and other professionals involved in the assessment of the patient, should give advice and assistance. They should not assist in a patient's detention unless they believe it is justified and lawful' (Code 17.11). If the nearest relative does make the application, e.g. where the AMHP disagrees with need or urgency for compulsory admission and the person is detained in hospital under section 2 or section 3, the hospital managers must request the relevant local authority to provide them with a social circumstances report (section 14).
- The nearest relative may make an application (section 11(1)), provided there are two valid medical recommendations, for the person to be received into guardianship (section 7). The nearest relative would complete form G1.
- The nearest relative can be consulted (section 11(4)(b)), whenever practicable, by an AMHP before a decision is made about a patient's possible compulsory admission to hospital for assessment (section 2) or for treatment (section 3).
- While there is no requirement for the nearest relative to be informed and consulted when a CTO is being considered, the Code 29.10 notes that 'consultation at an early stage with the patient and those involved in the patient's care will be important, including family and carers'.

- The nearest relative can formally object ((section 11(4), Code 14.65) to the making of an application by an AMHP for admission for treatment (section 3) or guardianship (section 7). If the nearest relative took this step, compulsory admission to hospital or reception into guardianship could not proceed at that time. The mental health professionals would in turn give urgent consideration to seeking the 'displacement' of the nearest relative in an application to the County Court (section 29(3)(c)).
- The nearest relative can order a patient's discharge (section 23)
  - from detention (section 2 or section 3), or
  - from a community treatment order (CTO) (section 17A) but only where the CTO followed detention under section 3. This would also discharge the suspended section 3 underpinning the CTO.
- The nearest relative must give 72 hours' notice in writing to the hospital. An illustrative standard letter for this purpose is given in the Code of Practice, paragraph 32.25. The nearest relative's order may be barred if within the 72 hours, the patient's responsible clinician provides a written report (M2) that they consider that the patient, if so discharged, 'would be likely to act in a manner dangerous to other persons or to himself' (section 25; regulation 25(1)(a) and (b), Mental Health Regulations 2008, and Code 32.20–32.25). The barring report prevents the nearest relative from ordering discharge at any time in the six months following the date of the report (section 25(1)(b), section 25(1A)). If the patient were detained under section 2, the nearest relative cannot take the matter further. If the patient is detained under section 3 or on a CTO following section 3, then the nearest relative may, within 28 days of the barring report being issued, apply to the Mental Health Tribunal for the patient's discharge instead (section 66(1)(g), section 66(2)(d)). For the situation when the matter is considered by the hospital managers panel, see Code 38.20.
- The nearest relative can order a patient's discharge (section 23) from guardianship (section 7). There is no power for the responsible clinician to bar discharge.
- Although they cannot order the discharge of a **Part III** CTO patient, the nearest relative can apply to the MHRT instead, in certain circumstances.
- The nearest relative should be given seven days' notice, if practicable, by the hospital before a patient is discharged from detention under sections 2 or 3 or from a CTO (section 133). This duty does not apply if the patient or the nearest relative has requested that this information should not be given.
- The functions of the nearest relative can be delegated to another person (Reg. 24, Mental Health Regulations, 2008, Code 5.5). There is no statutory form. Delegation must be in writing and could be an ordinary letter, e.g. 'I [insert name] of [insert address] being the nearest relative of [insert patient's name and address] for the purposes of the Mental Health Act 1983, hereby delegate my powers of nearest relative to [insert name] of [insert address]. I confirm that [insert name] has consented to act as the nearest relative of [insert patient's name].'

- As delegation could be time limited or until further notice, it is important that this issue is clearly addressed. It must also be signed and dated. Authorisation may be transmitted electronically (provided the new person is willing to receive it in that format). Delegation is not completed until received (and accepted) by the new person. The nearest relative must give notice of the delegation to the patient; the managers of the hospital if the person is detained and/or subject to a community treatment order; the local social services authority (and the private guardian, if any) if the person is subject to guardianship.

- Nearest relatives can apply to the First-tier Tribunal if they have been displaced by the County Court on the grounds of either an unreasonable objection to detention or guardianship (section 29(3)(c)) or exercising their power of discharge (section 23) from detention or a CTO (including where it is considered the nearest relative is likely to do so) 'without due regard to the welfare of the patient or the interests of the public' (section 29(3)(d)). Application can be made once in the first year following displacement and once in each subsequent year (section 29(6), section 66(1)(h), section 66(2)(g)). The acting nearest relative has a separate power to make an application.

- The patient or the nearest relative can apply to the Mental Health Tribunal for the patient's discharge when the patient is subject to an unrestricted hospital order (section 37) in the period between six and 12 months after the making of the hospital order and in any subsequent period of one year.

- The nearest relative can, in addition to the patient's own right, apply to the Mental Health Tribunal for discharge when the patient is subject to a guardianship order (section 37) within the first 12 months of the order and in any subsequent 12-month period (section 69(1)(b)(ii)).

Appendix 5 Brief guide to assessing children and young people

Practical issues

- Check if young person is known to children's services or Child and Adolescent Mental Health Services (CAMHS).
- If admission is likely, where would the bed be?
- Where is young person currently, are they in a safe and appropriate place?
- Do you have access to at least one CAMHS specialist for the assessment?

Place of safety issues

- A police station should never be used (unless a young person is so violent they can only be cared for safely in that environment).
- Even if the usual place of safety is within a facility for those over 18 years, this does not preclude a younger person being taken there. In these circumstances, ensure appropriate support is available to the young person.
- Remember, anywhere can be a place of safety, as long as those responsible are happy to have them there (e.g. a CAMHS ward).

Age-appropriate accommodation

- All under-18-year-olds should be admitted to accommodation 'appropriate to their age, subject to their needs'.
- This means even those not on section should not be admitted into an adult ward, unless their needs can only be met in an adult environment.
- On a temporary basis, being on an adult ward (with additional support) would still be better than being kept in a police cell.
- If an under-16-year-old has to be admitted into an adult ward, this is *not* illegal, but *is* a serious incident the Care Quality Commission would need to be notified about.

Nearest relative issues

- If the young person is on a care order or interim care order, the local authority will act as nearest relative.

- If there is a residence order (or equivalent) in place, the person with the order will be nearest relative.
- If someone has special guardianship, they will be nearest relative.
- If the young person is a ward of court, you *must* get the court's permission (nearest relative rights are suspended).
- A father will only be considered as nearest relative if he also has parental responsibility.

Parental responsibility issues

- Those with parental responsibility can agree to treatment and care that amounts to a deprivation of liberty for an under-16-year-old, as long as:
  - those with parental responsibility are acting reasonably and in the child's best interests;
  - it is a decision most parents would expect to make;
  - there isn't any disagreement between those with parental responsibility about what to do.
  - the child themselves doesn't object.
  - the treatment isn't particularly invasive.
- Those with parental responsibility cannot authorise a deprivation of liberty for an over-16-year-old.
- For a child on a care order, the local authority cannot authorise a deprivation of liberty.

Diagnostic issues

CAMHS doctors use different diagnostic categories, so look out for:

- emotional disorders (depression, anxiety, trauma, phobias, OCD);
- developmental disorders (learning disabilities, ADHD, autism);
- conduct disorders (often linked to adult personality disorders, depression and anxiety);
- relationship disorders (bullying, severe friend and family relationship problems, substance and alcohol misuse, problematic Internet use, reactive attachment disorder).

Some statistics

- Fifty per cent of all lifetime mental illnesses start by age 14 years.
- Seventy-five per cent of all lifetime mental illnesses start by the mid-20s.
- One in 10 of 5–15-year-olds have a diagnosable mental health problem.
- Of these, 1 in 5 have more than one main type disorder.

- Borderline personality disorder occurs in up to 22 per cent of adolescents and young adults receiving out-patient appointments.
- One in 10 children accessing CAMHS will have autism spectrum disorders (ASD).
- Seventy per cent of children with ASD will have a mental health concern at some stage of life.
- Forty per cent of children will have two or more mental health problems.

Children and young people with a learning disability are:

- 33 times more likely to have ASD than peers who do not have a learning disability;
- 8 times more likely to have ADHD;
- 6 times more likely to have a conduct disorder;
- 3 times more likely to experience schizophrenia.

Section 25 of the Children's Act:

- can only be used in certain (limited) circumstances to authorise deprivation of liberty primarily of under-16-year-olds;
- is issued by application to the court;
- does not provide authority to assess or treat a mental disorder if the child objects;
- only applies in secure children's homes.

With thanks to Janet Blair (CAMHS specialist and AMHP).

Appendix 6 Brief guide to assessing rough sleepers

The following are the key factors that all practitioners (outreach workers, approved mental health professionals, doctors, police, ambulance staff) should consider when assessing risks associated with sleeping rough.

Demographic factors

- Is the person's age, gender, sexual orientation, etc., likely to lead to an increase in concern about their vulnerability?

Current physical health

Is the person:

- in poor physical health?
- refusing to attend to their physical health needs?
- having difficulty accessing physical health care?
- using drugs or alcohol?
- maintaining adequate personal hygiene?
- accessing adequate food and drink?
- experiencing physical health problems which are being exacerbated by sleeping rough?

Current mental health

Is the person:

- actively isolating themselves?
- looking anxious or scared?
- confused and/or disorientated?
- talking aloud to themselves or others who are not there?
- withdrawn, slow in response or uncommunicative?
- angry, threatening and aggressive?
- refusing to attend to their mental health needs?
- having difficulty accessing mental health care?

Current or expected weather conditions

Does the person:

- have appropriate clothing for the weather conditions?
- have warm bedding?
- use day centres or other facilities to shelter from the weather?
- have a sleep site which is sheltered and dry?

Level of isolation

Is the person:

- isolating themselves from others?
- receiving support from other people sleeping rough or family and friends?
- avoiding services and support provided by homelessness services?
- likely to develop a trusting relationship that may lead to them accepting accommodation?
- sleeping in a safe sleep site?

Monitoring arrangements

- Is it possible to monitor the person effectively?
- Is it possible to implement a plan to reduce risk?
- Is joint working needed with other agencies such as day centres and street outreach teams?

Access to welfare benefits or other statutory support

Is the person:

- able to organise themselves to claim benefits?
- experiencing paranoid ideas that prevent them engaging in official processes?

Pattern of homelessness

- How long has the person been sleeping rough?
- Are they constantly moving from place to place?

These factors may provide a framework to refer the person sleeping rough on to appropriate services.

Adapted from Kemshall and Pritchard (1997).

Particular risks to consider when carrying out an MHA assessment (or a mental capacity assessment/best interests decision)

Be mindful of any potential risks associated with the sleep site. Try to arrange a meeting point for the assessing team that is well lit and not too isolated, as the assessment may need to take place early in the morning or late in the evening.

- Is the sleep site safe?
- Are there others with the person sleeping rough who may pose a risk?
- Are members of the public likely to get involved?
- Does the person have a history of violence?
- Does the person have a dog?
- Does the person have a weapon?

The ABC model of risk

When contacting the police, it may be useful to collate risk information under the headings below using this model. It is being adopted by the Metropolitan Police as a way of assessing risks to vulnerable people. It identifies five key areas to be assessed:

- *Appearance and atmosphere*: What the assessor first sees in a person in distress, including physical problems such as bleeding.
- *Behaviour*: What the person in distress is doing, and whether this is in keeping with the situation and their usual self.
- *Communication*: What the person in distress is saying and how they are saying it.
- *Danger*: Is the person in distress in danger and are their actions putting other people in danger?
- *Environment*: Where is the person in distress situated, and is anyone else there?

With thanks to the Mental Health & Rough Sleepers steering group, hosted by Pathways.

Tools and guidance

- http://www.pathway.org.uk/services/mental-health-guidance-advice/

Reference

Kemshall, H. and Pritchard, J. (1997) *Good Practice in Risk Assessment and Risk Management 2: Key Themes for Protection, Rights and Responsibilities.* London: Jessica Kingsley Publishers.

Appendix 7   Brief guide to assessing autistic people

Overview

Anyone can be autistic. Limiting stereotypes and characterisations of autism are slowly shifting. Around 1 in 57 children are autistic (Roman-Urrestarazu et al. 2021), figures likely to be (at least) matched in adulthood – though many older people may not have a formal diagnosis. Women and girls (Ratto et al. 2018) and people of colour face additional barriers to diagnosis (Begeer et al. 2009).

The DSM-5 refers to autism spectrum disorder (ASD). However, there is a strong preference in the autistic community to be referred to as 'autistic people' (Kenny et al. 2015; Gernsbacher 2017; Bury et al. 2020; Botha et al. 2021), as autism is central to identity, and it is perceived as a neurological difference rather than a deficit or disorder.

Autistic people have been characterised as being lacking in empathy. However, Milton's research into the 'double empathy problem' has shown that miscommunication between autistic and non-autistic people is mirrored. So non-autistic people find it challenging to empathise with autistic people, as autistic people find it challenging to empathise with non-autistic people. As the professional in this scenario, it is important to understand some of the additional barriers that autistic people might be experiencing and work to 'bridge the gap'. If you're a neurodivergent professional, you're one step ahead.

This section makes some recommendations for considerations when working with autistic people, but it's important to remember that everyone is an individual and what works for one person might not be suitable for someone else. Many of the recommendations included here will be beneficial for anyone, regardless of neurology.

Sensory and social processing

Sensory and social overwhelm can lead to or add to dysregulation. Dysregulation can result in a shutdown (freeze) or meltdown (fight/flight) response being activated. This is not a controlled or chosen response and can be scary and painful to experience.

Sensory processing differences are commonly experienced by autistic people (MacLennan et al. 2022). This might include sensitivity to:

- sound – including sound that others might not be able to hear, such as electricity or 'background' noise;

- lights and visual processing;
- smell;
- texture (including to clothing, seating, and other materials);
- taste;
- touch;
- and internal senses that support balance, coordination and internal messaging relating to hunger, temperature and feelings may also be affected.

People can be over-sensitive to some senses, and under-sensitive to others. Accommodations to the sensory environment can improve wellbeing, comfort and engagement – providing a calm and neutral environment with minimal sensory inputs is often a good approach.

Social and communication norms for autistic people differ from neurotypical norms. It is often more direct and literal.

Top tips

Sensory environment

i   Be aware of and reduce sensory-processing demands. Turn out/down artificial lights, reduce background noise (e.g. turning off noisy heaters, projectors or electrical items such as fans), reduce smells (including cleaning materials, perfumes, smoke, food).

ii   Reduce noise outside the room if possible – e.g. asking for quiet in the corridor.

iii   Create a predictable environment. Aim for a calm, consistent and safe space, e.g. reduce unexpected noise, ensure that people are not entering and leaving the space, do what you say, when you say you will do it.

iv   Ensure that you are calm and well-regulated to support co-regulation.

v   Limit the number of people in the room and/or asking questions.

Communication

i   Share questions in advance if possible. This may support understanding and facilitate processing.

ii   Be clear and explicit.

iii   Ask one question at a time.

iv   Allow plenty of processing time between statements and questions.

v   Sit next to the person. If this isn't possible, try not to sit directly opposite to reduce visual processing demands.

vi   Don't expect, request or force eye contact.

vii   Be aware that some people might 'stim', for example vocalisations, hand or body movements, or 'fidgeting'.

viii Some autistic people may have atypical body language or facial expressions.

ix Some autistic people may experience situational mutism. This can be a sign of overload. It can be helpful to reduce demands, and to offer alternatives to spoken communication (e.g. writing questions and answers).

x Provide a concise, written summary of what's been discussed and agreed and what will happen next.

Note: The Mental Health Act Review is considering the removal of autism and learning disabilities, without co-occurring mental health issues. However, as autistic people continue to be at increased risk of mental health challenges (Doherty et al. 2022), the approach suggested here will continue to be relevant though the Act may change.

This appendix has been written by Jill Corbyn, Director of Neurodiverse Connection. www.ndconnection.co.uk

Further reading:

https://www.boingboing.org.uk/wp-content/uploads/2022/09/More-than-words-supporting-effective-communication-with-autistic-people-in-health-care-settings.pdf

https://www.ndti.org.uk/assets/files/Its-not-rocket-science-V6.pdf
Further reading can be found on http://www.ndconnection.co.uk/

References

Begeer, S., Bouk, S.E., Boussaid, W. et al. (2009) Underdiagnosis and referral Bias of autism in ethnic minorities, *Journal of Autism and Developmental Disorders*, 39: 142–148. https://doi.org/10.1007/s10803-008-0611-5

Botha, M., Hanlon, J. and Williams, G.L. (2023) Does language matter? Identity-first versus person-first language use in autism research: A response to Vivanti, *Journal of Autism and Developmental Disorders*, 53: 870–78. https://doi.org/10.1007/s10803-020-04858-w

Bury, S.M., Jellett, R., Spoor, J.R. et al. (2023) "It defines who I am" or "It's something I have": What language do [autistic] Australian adults [on the autism spectrum] prefer? *Journal of Autism and Developmental Disorders*, 53: 677–87. https://doi.org/10.1007/s10803-020-04425-3

Crompton, C., DeBrabander, K., Heasman, B. et al. (2021) Double empathy: Why autistic people are often misunderstood, *Young Minds*, 9:554875. doi: 10.3389/frym.2021.554875

Doherty, M., Neilson, S., O'Sullivan, J., et al. (2022) Barriers to healthcare and self-reported adverse outcomes for autistic adults: A cross-sectional study. *BMJ Open*, 12:e056904. doi: 10.1136/bmjopen-2021-056904

Gernsbacher, M. (2017) Editorial perspective: The use of person-first language in scholarly writing may accentuate stigma, *The Journal of Child Psychology and Psychiatry*, https://doi.org/10.1111/jcpp.12706

Kenny, L., Hattersley, C., Moline, B. et al. (2015) Which terms should be used to describe autism? Perspective from the UK autism community, *Autism*, 1–20. DOI: 10.1177/1362361315588200

MacLennan, K., Woolley, C., Emily @21andsensory et al. (ahead of print) "It is a big spider web of things": Sensory experiences of autistic adults in public spaces, *Autism in Adulthood*, http://doi.org/10.1089/aut.2022.0024

Ratto, A.B., Kenworthy, L., Yerys, B.E., et al. (2018) What about the girls? Sex-based differences in autistic traits and adaptive skills, *Journal of Autism Development Disorders*, 48(5):1698–1711. doi: 10.1007/s10803-017-3413-9. PMID: 29204929; PMCID: PMC5925757

Roman-Urrestarazu, R. Van Kessel and Allison, C. (2021) Association of race/ethnicity and social disadvantage with autism prevalence in 7 million school children in england, *JAMA Pediatrics*, DOI: 10.1001/jamapediatrics.2021.0054

Example from practice

See example of Tony, given on page 83.

Introducing an assessment to an autistic person

Tony is autistic. He has auditory sensitivity and prefers clear and explicit language that he can easily understand. His auditory processing difficulties mean that it's helpful to have written communication to support what is being said.

The AMHP takes a deep breath to ensure they are calm, asks colleagues outside to keep noise down, and reminds them to close doors gently rather than letting them slam. She then enters the room and sits next to Tony, to reduce visual processing demands and so they can write notes as well as talking.

The lights in the room are very bright and it's not possible to reduce them. She notices this and acknowledges it and apologises that they can't be controlled. She tells Tony that she will meet with him for no more than 20 minutes, but that she will come back and see him later and talk to him about what will happen next.

She tells Tony that she will ask him some questions to find out if he is poorly, if he needs more support, or if he needs to have some time in hospital. She asks one question at a time and gives Tony space to consider what she has said and respond. She writes down her questions as she asks them and puts the pen down so Tony has the choice of writing and/or speaking his response.

Although still agitated, Tony's sensory needs have been understood and acknowledged and his communication preferences have been supported, facilitating his involvement in the process.

Neurodiverse Connection

Appendix 8 A Brief guide to using s135 and s136

Where do you need an s135 warrant?	Which definitely includes:	Places you don't need an s135 warrant:
'Any house, flat or room where that person, or any other person is living or any yard, garden, garage or outhouse that is used in connection with the house, flat or room, other than one that is also used in connection with one or more other houses flats or rooms' i.e. a **private dwelling**.	A place someone is living, and any associated buildings or places (like gardens or sheds) that are solely intended for use by those living there.	Places that are shared with other houses, rooms or flats, such as: communal gardens; communal hallways; shared entrances; rooftops; offices.
	Where can s136 definitely be used? • railway lines; • hospital wards; • rooftops (of commercial or business buildings); • police stations; • offices; • schools; • gardens and car parks associated with communal residential property; • non-residential parts of residential buildings with restricted entry.	
So where can a police officer use s136? Basically, anywhere that *isn't a private dwelling.*		**Places where it'll be up to the interpretation of the PC involved:** in the communal lounge in a residential home, a tent, a car, a hotel room.... (you get the idea)

Consultations for s136: The PC must consult a mental health professional before using s136 (if it's practical to do so)	Who could be the MH professional? • an approved mental health professional; • a registered nurse; • a registered medical practitioner; • an occupational therapist; • a paramedic.	What's the purpose of the consultation? To share information and advice about the person, and help the PC decide whether to use s136 (or decide on a different support plan) and where to go.
When does the time start? If you use s135 to stay in someone's home - when the PC entered the home.	If the person is *removed* to a place of safety under s135 or 136, when the person arrives *in* the place of safety. But time waiting to get to or into the place of safety doesn't count...	And if the police officer decides to 'keep' the person in another suitable place (for example, taking them to their home) when the PC makes that decision...

What counts as a place of safety? A place of safety is now defined in the Act as: • a hospital; • an independent hospital or care home for mentally disordered persons; • a police station; • residential accommodation provided by a local social services authority; • any other suitable place (with the consent of a person managing or residing at that place). **Which could be the person's own home.**	**But you can only use a person's own home as long as:** • the person you are assessing agrees; and • if others also live there, at least one of those people agree.

What 'agreeing' to conducting the assessment in a suitable place (like someone's home) means: 'it will be relevant whether the person can understand the information relevant to the decision, retain that information, use or weigh that information as part of the process of making the decision, and communicate that decision... The person must not however be coerced or pressured into giving such agreement or expressing a preference to remain at a private dwelling. If they are clearly unable to understand or communicate with police or mental health professionals, the necessary agreement cannot be sought or obtained.' p.15

How long does the s135/136 last?	When can the 24 hours be extended?	Who can extend the time?
24 hours, - which can be extended by up to 12 hours to a total of 36 hours. The extension can be agreed at anytime during the 24 hours.	The 24 hours can only be extended if is not practicable to complete a Mental Health Act assessment within the 24-hour period because of the person's condition (physical or mental).	The time can only be extended by the medical practitioner responsible for the person's **psychiatric** care - but if the person is being held in a police station, a superintendent (or above) must also agree to the extension.
And if the person goes AWOL whilst they are being transported to the place of safety, they may be retaken within 24 hours of the point when they went AWOL.	**If they go AWOL after arriving at the place of safety,** they can be retaken during the period of 'detention' left on the clock - including any extension of the 24 hours, that has already been agreed.	
Using a police station as a place of safety: should be exceptional- and it is now illegal for an under-18-year-old.	**You can use a police station as a POS as long as:** 1/ the person's behaviour evidences an imminent risk of serious injury or death; 2/ because of the behaviour, nowhere else can reasonably be expected to cope; 3/ so far as is reasonably practical, support from an MH professional will be available to the person; 4/ an inspector or more senior officer agree the plan.	

Glossary

Advance decision   A refusal of consent to a particular form of medical treatment that has been made while the person has capacity. Has statutory force but can be overridden by the Mental Health Act.

Advance statement   A request to be treated in a particular way. Does not have statutory force but needs to be taken into consideration.

Approved mental health professional (AMHP)   The AMHP is the applicant in the Mental Health Act Admission Process.

Approved clinician   An experienced professional (doctor, social worker, psychologist, nurse or occupational therapist) approved by a strategic health authority as possessing the necessary knowledge, skills and treatment to be able to be responsible for the care and treatment of someone cared for within the mental health system. Only an approved clinician who is also a registered medical practitioner (a doctor) is able to provide recommendations for admission to hospital under s2, s3 or s4 as well as guardianship. This is because only a doctor can *legally* provide a diagnosis.

Best interest assessor (BIA)   Has a key role in the DoLS process. With a specially trained doctor, the best interest assessor assesses people and makes decisions about whether or not a deprivation is in the best interests of the patient.

Capacity   The ability to make a decision about a particular matter at the time the decision needs to be made.

Case law   Judgements made in courts that provide new understanding of how to interpret the law itself.

Common law   Law derived from judicial decisions, i.e. High Court judges making decisions to cover situations where law does not currently exist. For example, until the Mental Capacity Act 2005 was passed by Parliament, most of the legislative framework used to support people who lacked capacity could be found in 'case law', i.e. the 'Common Law'.

Community treatment order (CTO)   A CTO is also sometimes referred to as Supervised Community Treatment or SCT. However, they both refer to the same thing – the ability to set conditions on the release from hospital for someone detained under s3, and the ability to recall that person to hospital if necessary. It is s17A of the Mental Health Act 1983.

Competent adults   All adults (those aged over 16 years) are presumed to have capacity or competence to make their own decisions, even if other people don't agree that the decision they want to make is 'wise'.

Compulsion   The term 'compulsion' is used as opposed to 'detention' to make clear that the Mental Health Act allows us to impose restrictions on people in the community as well as in hospital. However, we cannot deprive someone of their liberty in the community without seeking additional authority (for example, using a deprivation of liberty order). We can 'compel' people to live in a particular place, or allow people to see them at home, as well as 'compelling' them to take medication in hospital, even if they don't want to have it.

Court of protection   The Court of Protection has the same legal status as the High Court, and deals with any cases related to those who are over 16 years old where there are challenges linked to the Mental Capacity Act. For example, disputes around whether someone has capacity to make a decision, or what might be in their best interests.

Crisis resolution/home treatment approach (CRHT)   Most CRHT teams are multidisciplinary in nature, and include social workers, nurses and doctors. The aim of these teams (which exist in most parts of the country) is to provide people with the care and treatment they need in their own homes, and therefore avoid admission to hospital.

Delegation Making a decision to pass on or confer power owned by one person or organisation to another person or organisation. For example, a nearest relative can delegate their authority to be consulted about whether or not to use s3 with another person if they so wish.

Deputy A deputy of the Court of Protection, appointed to act on behalf of a person who lacks capacity.

Deprivation of Liberty Safeguards (DoLS) These amendments have been inserted into the Mental Capacity Act 2005, and provide a process by which it is now possible to authorise the detention of a person who lacks appropriate capacity, where that detention is the only way in which treatment can be provided, and is provided in the person's best interest.

Displacement The court process by which it is possible to replace a patient's nearest relative with someone else. The patient also has the right to apply for displacement.

Donee The person to whom powers are given under the Mental Capacity Act 2005, to act on the donor's behalf (for example, as the result of a Lasting Power of Attorney).

Gillick competence A 'Gillick competent child' is a child who has attained a sufficient understanding and intelligence to enable them to understand fully what is involved in a proposed intervention. In such circumstances, that child will also have the competence to consent to that intervention (CoP 36.38).

Guardianship Guardianship under the Mental Health Act comes under s7. It can only be used with people aged 16 or older, and provides the guardian with three specific powers: (1) the power to require the service user to live in a particular place (plus the power both to take the person there in the beginning, and return the person to that place if they leave without the guardian's permission); (2) the requirement that the service user to attend a place for 'treatment or occupation'; (3) the requirement that the service user let people visit them at home, as specified in the care plan. It provides an added level of authority, to make it more likely that a patient will comply with a care plan.

Health-based places of Safety (HBPoS) The name given to the place to which police can bring someone on an s135 or s136.

Independent mental capacity advocate (IMCA) A role created by the Mental Capacity Act 2005 to make sure people who lack capacity, and who have no one else to speak up on their behalf, have someone to step in to take part in decisions about major issues.

Independent mental health advocate (IMHA) A role created by the Mental Health Act 2007 to ensure anyone subject to detention (except those detained on short-term sections such as an s5(2) or s136) understands and exercises their rights.

Lasting Power of Attorney (LPA) These powers were created under the Mental Capacity Act 2005. They replace Enduring Powers of Attorney (although existing EPAs are still valid), and unlike the EPA, can be used not only to appoint someone to look after the person's money once they lose capacity, but also to make decisions about welfare and medical treatment on behalf of the patient.

Liability When you are legally responsible for something.

Liable to be detained Once recommendations have been signed and an application has been made, the person is 'liable to be detained' (i.e. the power exists to take them to hospital, by force if necessary).

Liberty Protection Safeguards (LPS) were proposed to replace DoLS. There are currently no plans to bring them into force.

Ordinary residence 'Ordinary residence' is legally defined as the place where the patient would normally consider themselves as living 'for a settled purpose'. So for someone in hospital or residential care, their place of ordinary residence will be the place they lived prior to admission even if they move to a new area on discharge. However, this does not apply if the patient is re-detained on an s3. In this case, the place of ordinary residence (and therefore right of access to free services under s117) will fall on the area where the person lived prior to the new admission.

Parental responsibility (PR)   This term is defined in the Children Act 1989 as 'all the rights, duties, powers, responsibilities and authority which by law a parent has in relation to a child and his property' (s3(1) Children Act 1989 – this Act defines a child as aged under 18).

Part III   Part III patients are subject to compulsion by virtue of forensic sections of the Mental Health Act, i.e. they were placed on their sections by the courts.

Primary legislation   Acts debated and passed by Parliament.

Ratified   When a treaty or convention is officially sanctioned by Parliament.

Registered medical practitioner   A doctor who has completed necessary qualifications and is licensed to practise as a medical doctor.

Responsible clinician (RC)   The role taken by an experienced professional who has completed 'approved clinician training'. Only people subject to compulsion under the Mental Health Act have an allocated 'responsible clinician'. It is the responsible clinician who makes decisions related to the use of compulsion, such as whether someone should stay on section or be discharged, whether they are well enough to have s17 leave, and so on.

Systemic risk assessment   This involves considering risks from a range of perspectives, to ensure that when making a decision, it is informed by all the facts of the case.

Unrestricted forensic section   'Unrestricted' forensic sections are those where the courts have not imposed particular requirements on the patients. Usually this occurs using s41 MHA.

Vicarious liability   Liability of an organisation for the actions or inactions of its employees, agents or volunteers.

References and useful resources

Department of Education (2015) *Information Sharing: Guidance for Practitioners and Managers*. London: HM Government.

Department of Health (2009) *The Legal Aspects of the Care and Treatment of Children and Young People with Mental Disorder: A Guide for Professionals*. London: National Institute for Mental Health in England.

Department of Health (2015) *Code of Practice Mental Health Act 1983*. London: The Stationery Office.

Department of Health (2015) *Reference Guide to the Mental Health Act 1983*. London: The Stationery Office.

Equality and Human Rights Commission (2023) *The Essential Guide to the Public Sector Equality Duty*. London: The Equality and Human Rights Commission.

Home Office and DHSC (2017) *Guidance for the implementation of changes to police powers and places of safety provisions in the mental health act 1983*.

Index

admission criteria, Mental Health Act
    1983 (MHA) 90
  appropriate in all the circumstances
    102–4
  appropriate treatment (s3) 100–2
  deprivation of liberty or MHA 97
  drugs & alcohol exclusion 91–2
  health or safety 94–6
  informal admission 98
  learning disability qualification
    92–3
  mental disorder 90–3
  nature or degree 93–4
  no alternative to hospital admission
    96–102
admission to hospital
  actions on admission 128–9
  admitting nurses' checklist 130
  conflicts of interest – checking 130
  correctable and non correctable faults
    126–7
  electronic forms 127–8
  forms checklist 130
  outline report – AMHP 129
  outline report – Doctor 164
  patient rights -s132 129
  no admission - no bed 111
  no admission - not needed 109
  telling the nearest relative 111
  telling people 108
advanced decisions, refusing medical
    treatment 15–17, 60–1
  Community Treatment Orders (CTO) 16
  ECT 16
  Lasting Powers of Attorney (LPA) 17
advanced statements 15
AMHP see Approved Mental Health
    Professional
appropriateness, admission criteria,
    Mental Health Act 1983 (MHA)
    102–3
Approved Mental Health Professional
    (AMHP)
  CTO, role in 147–8
  conveyance to hospital 118–125
  guardianship, role in 139–140

report, AMHP outline report 129,
    164–5
Asperger's Syndrome
  Mental Health Act assessments 93
Autistic Spectrum Disorders, Mental
    Health Act assessments 92–3
  brief guide to assessing autistic people
    175–7

beds, finding, Mental Health Act
    assessments 77–8

children and young people 11–15
  brief guide to assessing children &
    young people 168–170
  Children Act 12
  deprivation of liberty 12
  Gillick competent 14
  informal admission 15
  local authority 13
  parental responsibility scope of
    12–14
  parental responsibility 19
choosing between sections and Acts
    104–7
Code of Practice see MHA Code of
    Practice (CoP)
Community Treatment Orders (CTO)
    144–154
  AMHP role 147–8
  application process 144–5
  AWOL 150
  conditions 146
  criteria 145–6
  effect of CTO 148
  extending CTO 149–150
  length of CTO 148
  MCA interface issues 149
  pros and cons 153–4
  protections 149
  recall 150–151
  responsible clinician role 144–5
  revocation 153
  treatment in the community 148
  which AMHP? 147
  s136 & urgent presentations 152

compulsion in the community 132–158
  Community Treatment Orders (CTO)
    144–154
  CTO or long term leave 134
  different powers – comparison 132–5
  deprivation of liberty - authorising
    community deprivation of liberty 133
  deprivation of liberty safeguards 154–8
conflicts of interests 69–71
consultations
  nearest relative 54–7
  other people 58–60
conveyance to hospital 50, 117–125
  actions following arrival, AMHP 128–9
  Approved Mental Health Professional
    (AMHP) 118–123
  checklist, final arrangements 124–5
  delegating 118–9
  electronic forms 127–8
  escorting 120–1
  evidencing problems 122
  long distance 122–3
  managing 119–120
  paperwork 124
  powers, guidance on 123
  receiving nurses 125–7
  timing 121
CoP see MHA Code of Practice
Crisis Resolution / Home Treatment
  (CRHT) Mental Health Act
  assessments 29–31
criteria for admission see admission criteria,
  Mental Health Act 1983 (MHA)
CTO see Community Treatment Orders

decisions, implementing 108–130
delegating, conveyance to hospital
  118–9
delegating, nearest relative (NR)
  functions 62–3
deprivation of liberty - concept
  meaning 3
  impact on MHAA 98–100
Deprivation of Liberty Safeguards (DoLS)
  154–8
  advantages/disadvantages 157–8
  application process 154–5
  assessment process 155–6
  community DoLS 158
  criteria 156–7
  deciding between MHA and DoLS 158
  treatment rules 157

displacement, nearest relative (NR)
  functions 63–8
doctors, s12 approved 71–2
DoLS see Deprivation of Liberty
  Safeguards

ECHR see European Convention on
  Human Rights
emergency admissions, s4
  Mental Health Act assessments
    36–37
Equality Act 2010 4–5
European Convention on Human Rights
  (ECHR) 2–3
extended s17 leave, longer term care
  133–5

four step test, Mental Capacity Act
  2005(MCA) 8

Gillick competent, children and young
  people 14
glossary 181–3
guardianship 135–44
  absent without leave (AWOL) 141
  application process 136–7
  Approved Mental Health Professional
    (AMHP) Role 139–40
  care planning 140
  criteria 137–9
  doctor's role 139
  ending 141–2
  Mental Capacity Act 2005 (MCA)
    interface issues 142
  renewal process 141
  safeguards 140–1
  timescales 140–1
  transfer back to hospital 142

health/safety, admission criteria,
  Mental Health Act 1983 (MHA)
  93–4
home treatment see Crisis Resolution/
  Home Treatment
hospital admissions see admission
  criteria, Mental Health Act
  1983; admission to hospital,
  implementing
hospital, conveyance see conveyance to
  hospital
hospital managers section papers
  checklist 161–2

Human Rights Act 1998 (HRA) 2–5
    Article 5 2–4
    children and young people 11–12
    effect on mental health legislation 2–4

identification of nearest relative 51–4
IMHA (Independent Mental Health Advocate)
    checklist 76
    Mental Health Act assessments 73–6
informal admission, Mental Capacity Act
        2005 (MCA) 98
information sharing 26–7
interpreting when interviewing 85–7
implementing decisions 108–130
    applications 115–17
    medical recommendations 112–15
    not admitting / no bed / more time
        109–12
    telling people the outcome 108–9
    timescales 162
    conveyance see conveyance to hospital

judging risk and urgency, Mental Health
        Act assessments 27–29

Lasting Power of Attorney (LPA) 17
leave of absence, extended leave 138–40
legal frameworks, children and young
        people 14–15
local contacts, specialist groups of
        patients 159–60
longer term care see compulsion in the
        community
LPA see Lasting Powers of Attorney

MCA see Mental Capacity Act 2005
medical recommendations, admission to
        hospital see implementing
Mental Capacity Act 2005 (MCA)
    age requirements 5
    best interest checklist 8–9
    care and treatment 18
    children and young people 5
    Deprivation of Liberty Safeguards
        (DoLS) 156
    definitions 5,7
    four step test 8
    guardianship 142
    informal treatment 18, 27
    key concepts 6
    Lasting Power of Attorney (LPA) 17
    limitations 10–11
    mental capacity, defining 7

    principles 6–7
    protection from liability 9–10
    responsibility for testing capacity 8
    testing for capacity, four stage test 8
mental disorder, admission criteria Mental
        Health Act assessments see
        admission criteria
Mental Health Act assessments
    alternatives 29–31
    appropriate assessors 68
    Aspergers Syndrome 91, 137
    Autistic Spectrum Disorder, brief guide
        186
    beds 76-8
    children and young persons 18 years or
        younger 11–14
    choosing between acts 106–7
    choosing between sects 104–6
    in the community 38–51
    co-ordinating the process 80–7
    conflicts of interest 69–71
    considering the need for assessment 36
    deciding between the MHA and DoLS 158
    emergency admissions 36–7
    explanations 82–3
    gathering information 25
    Independent Mental Health Advocate
        (IMHA) 73–6
    information gathering 58–60
    interpreting 85–7
    introductions 82–3
    judging risk and urgency 27–9
    learning disability qualification 92–3
    managing Risks 80–2
    medical (psychiatric) assessment 84–5
    mental disorder 90–2
    nearest relative (NR) 54–8
    nature or degree 93–4
    participation of person 20–1
    place of safety (definition) 62
    police custody 23
    public place detaining see s136
    starting assessment 81
    systemic risk assessment 28
    team makeup 68–73
MHA see Mental Health Act 1983
MHA Code of Practice (CoP) 18–21
    principles 19–20
    status 19

nature or degree, admission criteria,
        Mental Health Act 1983 (MHA)
        93–4

nearest relative (NR) 51–4
  consultation 54–6
  delegating functions 62–3
  displacing NR 63–8
  good enough consultation 54
  identifying 51–4
  informing and consulting 55
  not practicable to consulting 54, 56–7
  ordinary residence rule 51–2
  rights 51, 165–67
  talking to other people 58
no alternative, admission criteria, Mental
    Health Act 1983 (MHA) 96–102
NR see nearest relative
no authority to detain
  managing situations 32–3
  no bed 111

recall, CTO 150–52
refusing medical treatment
  advance decisions 15–17
relative, nearest see nearest relative (NR)
removal to a place of safety 41
report, sample AMHP outline report
    163–4
report, sample doctors report 164
revocation, CTO 153
risk, judging risk and urgency 27–9
risk management
  children and young people 29
rough sleepers, brief guide to assessment
    171–3

safeguards, guardianship 140–1
safety/health, admission criteria, Mental
    Health Act 1983 94–6
Sections - admission & treatment
  s2 88
  s3 88
Sections - community powers
  CTO - s17 89
  deprivation of liberty – MCA 89
  guardianship s7 89
Sections – other
  s115 82
Sections - short term 87–8
  s4(emergency admission) 36–7
  s5/2 34–6
  s5/4 33–4
  s135(1) 42–9
  s136 38–42
  brief guide to using s135 and s1361
    78–80
systemic risk assessment 27–9

team makeup, Mental Health Act
    assessments 68–73
  checklist 72–3
  conflict of interest 69–71
timescales, guardianship 140–1
transfer back to hospital, guardianship
    142
transport to the place of safety 50

urgency, judging risk and urgency 27–9

www.ingramcontent.com/pod-product-compliance
Lightning Source LLC
Chambersburg PA
CBHW070332270326
41926CB00017B/3851